DEVELOPING
TRANSFERABLE
SKILLS

SUCCESS IN RESEARCH

The Success in Research series has been designed by Cindy Becker and Pam Denicolo to provide short, authoritative and accessible guides for students, researchers and academics on the key area of professional and research development.

Each book is written with an eye to avoiding jargon and each aims to cut to the chase of what readers really need to know about a given topic. These are practical and supportive books and will be essential reading for any students or researchers interested in developing their skills and broadening their professional and methodological knowledge in an academic context.

SUCCESS IN RESEARCH

DEVELOPING TRANSFERABLE SKILLS

ENHANCING YOUR RESEARCH AND EMPLOYMENT POTENTIAL

PAM DENICOLO ♀ JULIE REEVES

Los Angeles | London | New Delhi
Singapore | Washington DC

Los Angeles | London | New Delhi
Singapore | Washington DC

SAGE Publications Ltd
1 Oliver's Yard
55 City Road
London EC1Y 1SP

SAGE Publications Inc.
2455 Teller Road
Thousand Oaks, California 91320

SAGE Publications India Pvt Ltd
B 1/I 1 Mohan Cooperative Industrial Area
Mathura Road
New Delhi 110 044

SAGE Publications Asia-Pacific Pte Ltd
3 Church Street
#10-04 Samsung Hub
Singapore 049483

Editor: Katie Metzler
Assistant editor: Anna Horvai
Production editor: Ian Antcliff
Copyeditor: Sarah Bury
Proofreader: Louise Harnby
Marketing manager: Catherine Slinn
Cover design: Shaun Mercier
Typeset by: C&M Digitals (P) Ltd, Chennai, India
Printed in Great Britain by Henry Ling Limited,
at the Dorset Press, Dorchester, DT1 1HD

Library of Congress Control Number: 2013940254

British Library Cataloguing in Publication data

A catalogue record for this book is available from the
British Library

MIX
Paper from
responsible sources
FSC™ C013985
www.fsc.org

ISBN 978-1-4462-6033-3
ISBN 978-1-4462-6034-0 (pbk)

To *all* of the researchers who have inspired and taught us over the years, and to the colleagues, mentors and fellow 'Roberts' developers who have supported, encouraged and stretched us. The Roberts agenda was a bold step and we are grateful to the late Sir Gareth Roberts, the decision makers and people who had the vision to make it happen.

CONTENTS

LIST OF BOXES

LIST OF ACTIVITIES

LIST OF FIGURES

ABOUT THE AUTHORS AND ACKNOWLEDGEMENTS

Pam Denicolo, a chartered psychologist, recently retired from her full-time role at the University of Reading, where she developed the Graduate School system and the post-registration professional practice and postgraduate research element of the School of Pharmacy. As Emeritus Professor she maintains there a research group focusing on constructivist approaches to research while also having a part-time professorial role at the University of Surrey, advising on matters pertaining to doctoral studies derived from her research and professional experience. She provides similar consultancy advice and training workshops for researchers, supervisors and examiners for Higher Education Institutions (HEIs) in the UK and worldwide.

Her passion for supporting and developing graduate students is demonstrated through her contributions as Vice Chair to the UK Council for Graduate Education Executive Committee, as Chair of the Society for Research into Higher Education Postgraduate Network and Executive Editor of the Guides for Supervisors Series, and as a member of other national committees and working groups which, for example, review and evaluate the impact of the Roberts-funded generic skills training, and the concordance of UK universities with the European Code and Charter. She was a key contributor to Vitae's development of the Researcher Development Framework (RDF) and the QAA's Doctoral Characteristics Advisory Group and the group revising the Code of Practice section on postgraduate research.

Julie Reeves has been delivering skills training to researchers since 2005. Currently based at the University of Southampton, Julie designs, delivers and coordinates transferable skills training for early career researchers and research staff. Prior to this she was the Skills Training Manager, at the University of Manchester, for social science, arts and humanities postgraduate researchers, their supervisors and research staff. Her academic background is in politics and international relations, with degrees from the Universities of Kent and Southampton. Her PhD was on 'culture and international relations' and she maintains a keen interest in the internationalisation of education.

She held a Visiting Faculty Fellowship with the Civic Education Project, teaching international relations in Belarus and Ukraine. She has had a varied career, working in the public, private and education sectors. A stint as a cook on an Australian cattle station led to one of her all-time transferable skills achievements: she invented the corned-beef pizza! She is a member of the Chartered Institute of Personnel and Development and a convenor of the Society for Research into Higher Education's Postgraduate Issues Network.

Julie met Pam through Vitae, as a member of the 'clustering and gap analysis group' for the 'Researcher Development Framework' (RDF). Since then they have shared their passion and enthusiasm for researchers, negotiated perspectives and drawn on their respective networks in an active personification of the advice they provide in this book.

They are grateful to the following for their expert contributions to this book, which gave it added zest as well as credibility.

Dawn Duke, leader of the University of Surrey Researcher Development team, produced Chapter 9 and convinced several of her colleagues to provide extracts of their wisdom.

Moira Bent, Faculty Librarian and National Teaching Fellow, Newcastle University, contributed substantially to the sections in Chapter 5 on information literacy.

Ellen Pearce, Director of Vitae, provided the section on the Researcher Development Planner in Chapter 2.

Janet Pink, Janet Pink Training Coaching & Consultancy, provided the Employability Skills questionnaire.

Tania-Morgan Alcantarilla, University of Southampton, contributed the Career planner.

Pam Morgan, Steve Hutchinson, Mike Rawlins discussed leadership and other topics with Julie.

PROLOGUE: WHY WE THINK THIS BOOK MAY BE USEFUL AND HOW YOU MIGHT ENGAGE WITH IT

Rationale for book, intended readership and use of terms

Our research careers have involved us in conducting research projects related to our disciplines and to researcher development and in working with a range of research colleagues, new and experienced, to improve their practice. During that time we have seen support for research practice progress from being restricted to local, collegial apprenticeship-type models to national and international initiatives which include a proliferation of support providers, codes of practice, quality codes, and charters/concordats. There is, though, at this point, no written summary of the situation for those newly embarking on or in the early stages of a research career, to guide them through professional expectations and opportunities in relation to skill development. These researchers are the prime audience for this book.

As new initiatives emerged and grew, so the vocabulary used to describe researchers has changed. It is now perceived to be much more fitting to describe those studying for a doctorate as postgraduate or doctoral researchers, while those employed in the few years after doctoral study are variously called postdocs, research staff or early career researchers. For simplicity, in this book we will use respectively the terms postgraduate researchers (PGRs) and early career researchers (ECRs) or refer to the early stages of a research career.

Another gradual change has occurred in the sector related to research careers. In the past it was assumed that the majority of those holding a doctorate would remain in the Higher Education sector as academic or research staff, the former combining research with teaching duties. Now the proportion of those remaining in academe is very much reduced, with doctoral degree holders being employed in a wide variety of professions and in roles which may be predominantly research-based or in which research approaches and skills are used in a multitude of other tasks. The range and quality of skills researchers possess (the skill set) have thus risen in importance and this has, in turn, placed greater emphasis on the training of researchers in the early part of their careers.

Although Higher Education Institutions (HEIs) strive to keep the essence of the doctorate unsullied, these changes in the general context of doctoral education and research inevitably lead to developments in practice which impinge on research supervisors and Principal Investigators (PIs), staff developers, research trainers/developers, librarians, careers staff, and so on. These people, too, might find this book useful. It is intended to help PGRs/ECRs, and those who support them, to become conversant with the philosophy and ideas behind one particular development, the high-lighting of transferable skills within doctoral education (as in other stages of education) and the first few years of postdoctoral research. The book covers how these skills can be identified, acquired, curated, assessed and evaluated, and then marketed to enhance career and employability pros-pects beyond the doctorate, whether that career is in Higher Education or other contexts, including or excluding further research.

A question of focus

The book begins by providing a general definition of the topic (generic, transferable skills) and provides a digest of the historical path that led to their current key role in researcher training as a means to enhance employability. Although we may all suspect that this was mainly initiated by political and economic motives, we can identify a wide range of ben-efits to PGRs/ECRs from engaging with this development, and some may see societal benefits also; yet its adoption has not been unproblematic. Changing well-established traditions is never easy. Nevertheless, the term 'generic/transferable skills' has entered the everyday vocabulary of Higher Education and associated organisations in recent years and is becoming recognised and used by employers as being the professional attributes sought in new recruits.

A new term implies that these are a new set of skills that researchers must acquire in addition to those traditionally developed in the first stages of their careers. In the vast majority of cases this is a misconception because the skills referred to have always been required to some extent to complete research work effectively, although previously they have been overshadowed by the knowledge and written product of the research, a thesis (or dissertation). Just as the figure and background are inseparable in the well-known Gestalt figure in Figure P.1 (below) – both the faces and vase are interdependent and present simultaneously – so the skills of research practice and the research product too are inseparable, but each can only be seen clearly by shifting focus. In the past, the focus was on the production of new knowledge demonstrated in the form of a thesis, with the development of a competent researcher being implicit as part of the process; now that development is more explicit.

Paradoxically, one professional skill previously neglected at master's/doctoral level was that of identifying and communicating one's transferable skills! In Chapter 1 we will note other omissions that might occur from any researcher's skill set because of disciplinary or institutional traditions, custom and practice as we trace the historical upsurge of interest in skills. From then onwards our focus will adjust so that transferable skills become the figure and the knowledge product the background of our discussion – still recognising that they co-exist and complement each other. We will recognise the value of developing those skills in early forays into research but will also acknowledge and

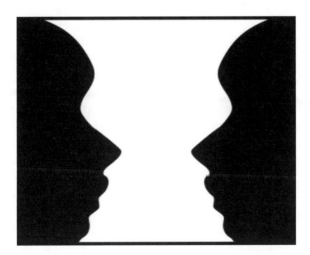

FIGURE P.1 Gestalt figure

appreciate that skills development is an ongoing process – a lifelong learning aspect of a career.

Your engagement with this book

Each of you as readers will come to this book with a range of prior experience and current needs. Although throughout the book we refer to you as if you were somewhere in the early stages of your research career, we do recognise that some of you may be more experienced in research. We thus provide below an outline of each chapter to help you select which ones will be most useful for your own needs. So, for instance, if you have already been immersed in the research aspects of Higher Education for some time you may well be aware of the changes in emphasis and practice that provide the context to professional skills development and need only to skim through Chapter 1 to check on such things as how we are defining terms. On the other hand, as a relative newcomer you may be interested to learn why and how new emphases have come about. In the latter case you may find Chapter 1 helps make sense of the situation.

Further, please note that this book is about transferable skills: their context, identification, means to their acquisition, how they can be monitored and marketed, and so on. It is not intended to be an encapsulated means of acquiring all transferable skills. Thus the first three chapters set the context, describing why they are needed, and how they can be identified and acquired, while in the chapters devoted to identifying specific groups of skills (Chapters 4, 5, 6, and 7) our purpose is to provide ideas and guidance about how and where they can be learnt rather than to teach the skills *per se*, although occasionally we do provide some learning exercises to get you started. Chapter 8 focuses on providing evidence of your skill set and monitoring progress, while Chapters 9 and 10 specifically link your skill development to employment. Finally, in Chapter 11 we provide advice about making skill development part of your normal life.

All of the contributors to this book are convinced that active learning is more effective than simply reading, so we have also tried to incorporate activities that will aid your preparation for future employment applications. Another part of active learning, and an important skill to cultivate, is reflection on action and experience; therefore we include suggestions for reflection throughout the book. Within chapters you will also find boxes that summarise key information that you might use again later when reviewing your ideas, while at the end of chapters we provide guidance on further reading or useful websites.

Outline of the book

Chapter 1   What are transferable skills and why they are needed?

A key message of the book is that transferable skills enhance research practice and the researcher, while the changing environment of research and practice means that specialist research skills alone are insufficient to ensure success in current research and any future career. This chapter includes an introduction to the significant changes in institutional practice in the UK, as an example, that have occurred since the Roberts Report 2002 in response to employers' requirements, including Higher Education employers. In such contexts, all researchers need to evaluate and extend their transferable skills, with the study of a doctorate providing an imperative but also an ideal opportunity to do so.

This introductory chapter puts transferable skills into the wider context, demonstrating that a person's prior experience contributes to research a source of transferable skills while other skills may require development over a longer timeframe. Recognising that researchers have diverse backgrounds and will have had different opportunities to develop certain key transferable skills, a summary is provided of the kind of skills that are in focus and more widely required, for example those that are generic rather than those relating to a subject/discipline or specific research project, and a working definition is provided.

Chapter 2   How can researchers identify which transferable skills are needed?

This chapter includes activities to enable the reader to identify some of their current skills and reflect on those that they might like to enhance or acquire. This will introduce the principles of development/training/learning needs analysis, through the process of experiencing these techniques for themselves. Reference is made to the Researcher Development Framework (RDF) and Statement (RDS). The RDF professional development planner, among other examples of logs or records of skill development; is introduced and described. The ensuing discussion includes how such tools can be used in future for self-development throughout a person's career.

Chapter 3   How can transferable skills be acquired?

It is not all about courses! Methods from self-study to formal accredited courses are discussed, with their strengths and weaknesses for particular skill groups and situations. This chapter seeks to help the reader to consider alternative ways of meeting development needs in order to close skills gaps while being smart and strategic about it. The distinction is drawn between skills learnt during the process of research and those derived from a variety of other experiences, activities and sources which could be re-oriented and brought to bear in research activities or environments. This will raise awareness of the broader requirements of research and how such skills are useful in a large range of settings beyond the academy. Motivational issues and individual learning styles are also considered.

Chapter 4   What are the key intellectual skills directly related to research?

This chapter deals with those skills acquired as part of engaging with the research project. Points are drawn out about the different skills acquired during the development of projects in the different disciplines, showing commonality and variation, and opportunities that may be explicit or hidden for cross-disciplinary enrichment. Sub-sections include the following, with related activities to help readers build on and broaden their initial skill set: subject knowledge and cognitive skills; research methods; academic literacy and numeracy; languages.

Chapter 5   What skills are involved in dealing with information and with maintaining integrity as a researcher?

This chapter focuses on information literacy and data management, with other sections addressing library skills, intellectual property rights (IPR), and key legal acts related to the use and disclosure of information, melding important factual information with discussion of practical applications. Similarly, the philosophical concepts of ethics and professional integrity are addressed with consideration of how they manifest themselves in research through, for instance, attribution and co-authorship issues.

Chapter 6   What are the key practical research project skills?

This chapter addresses those skills that may be acquired from research and are useful in other work and leisure contexts. It illustrates the transferability of such skills, and how they might be tailored to suit different environments, audiences and requirements. It will seek to remind readers that even apparently mundane and disparate activities can be viewed from different perspectives for translation into the world of work.

The practical skill areas discussed in this chapter include communication skills, networking, building reputation, managing health and safety issues, project and time management.

Chapter 7   What are the key people skills and personal attributes?

This chapter deals with what are sometimes referred to as the 'softer' skills, those associated with people and personal development which it would be advantageous to acquire in addition to the intellectual and practical skills derived directly from research. It makes reference to nurturing personal attributes as well as skills that make you an engaging, and engage-able, work colleague.

The topics covered include diversity and environmental awareness, leadership and people management skills, team working and other collaborative working skills in addition to how to be personally effective and to survive socially and politically.

Chapter 8   How can skill development be evidenced, assessed and evaluated?

This chapter considers different approaches to monitoring and evaluating progress in skill development, from formal assessment to the use of set objectives and evidence collection. The importance of different phases and career stages of development, and workplace transfer, is raised. Issues of quality as well as quantity of development and 'return on investment' are considered and the concept of continuing improvement and professional development plans are explored. A variety of ways to keep track of and exhibit development using different media are presented.

Chapter 9   How can transferable skills be marketed effectively to enhance employability?

This chapter concentrates on issues such as identifying audience needs and responding to them in a language and style that is appropriate, whether the audience is a prospective employer in or outside academe. The point is made in this chapter that different groups will be interested in different aspects of a skill set. The techniques promoted in this section will serve a variety of situations in which one has to 'sell' one's research outputs or oneself, for instance adapting a CV or portfolio for different purposes and presenting your skills in interview.

Chapter 10 How can researchers make a successful transition to another employment?

This chapter serves to alert readers to issues of transition and the challenges sometimes faced when working to different expectations or within different employment cultures. The habits acquired in an academic environment may not necessarily be appropriate and appreciated in others, while different modes of expression may be required for face-to-face encounters and in written material. Readers are encouraged by examples and activities to explore the etiquette of different work cultures.

Chapter 11 How can transferable skills become an integral part of life?

This chapter discusses managing your career and provides some tailored advice for specific cohorts. It emphasises building a CV through experimentation with a range of activities that develop wider research and world-related skills. It concludes the book by considering the continued development of your skill set as a professional through a process of lifelong learning.

Glossary of Terms

Some of the key terms that are regularly used in research training and researcher development are explained in this section.

1

WHAT ARE TRANSFERABLE SKILLS AND WHY THEY ARE NEEDED?

Chapter overview

This chapter reviews the:

- Skills that people bring to doctoral study
- Further skill requirements with a working definition of transferable skills
- Context: the history of change in doctoral education
- Particular developments in relation to training during and beyond the doctorate
- Consequences for careers beyond the doctorate
- Impact on the people involved: researchers, supervisors, trainers and other support staff

Skills at the commencement of the doctorate

Since the doctorate is the pinnacle of award-bearing courses in Higher Education, all those starting a doctorate will already have many relevant skills to bring to bear on the task – indeed, they will have been selected by the university because they have demonstrated some of those skills and have shown potential for developing others. Some will be very confident that they already have most of the required skills, while others may face with trepidation the requirement to conduct research that will 'make an original contribution to knowledge'. This demonstrates the wide variation in those who embark on doctoral studies, which is reflected also in the range and diversity of skills that each individual brings to the task, although it is not always the most confident who are the most skilled.

Over the last two decades the variety in student background has increased, as has the range of doctoral degrees to which they can address themselves. Not only is the gender ratio more balanced (although there continues to be some disciplinary differences), but those seeking qualification through Professional Doctorates have added to the number of more mature, and hence more experienced, doctoral researchers, studying full- or part-time. They often bring more employment-related skills to the task but do not always recognise their value, whereas those with more recent experience in Higher Education tend to have what we might call 'knowledge of the system' and more practised academic skills.

You, the reader, may be just embarking on a doctorate, or on your way to completing it and wondering about your career beyond the conferment of your degree, or be involved with postdoctoral research and looking to move on with your career. At this point you might like to begin to consider the skills you already have that you think you might need for the next stage or those that will enhance your career prospects overall. As you work your way through this book, you will find we suggest that you engage in some activities that will help you to clarify just what skills you do have and how you might strengthen, expand and harness them in pursuing your career. We suspect that you will have more appropriate and useful attitudes, abilities and aptitudes than you may think at this moment, but it might give you confidence to begin to identify some of your potential right away by trying Activity 1.1, which explores your skills beyond those learned in school and academia.

ACTIVITY 1.1   A FIRST LIST OF POTENTIALLY TRANSFERABLE SKILLS

Think back over any full- or part-time jobs that you have had, including vacation jobs or those to earn pocket money while you were still at school. List the skills that you brought to bear in them.

Then think of the hobbies you have or have had. Did they develop any skills that you could add to your list?

When we discussed our own experiences related to this, we recognised the cultivation of general attributes, such as time keeping and being organised, and some specific skills, for instance, that vacation jobs like waiting tables or bartending developed our skills of handling difficult people and multi-tasking, while hobbies such as gardening developed project planning, experimentation and many others that may not have seemed obvious at the time. Thus we feel sure that everyone reading this already has many skills, some in embryonic form and others that need re-orientating to fit different circumstances, but a range of useful skills nevertheless.

A first look at skills required during the doctorate

You may be wondering why we did not start by emphasising obvious academic skills since these will clearly be key ones for doctoral study, or perhaps you suspect that academic and 'generic/transferable skills' are beasts of different kinds. Let us allay that suspicion and agree that academic skills are part of the transferable skills family, as you will see in much more detail in Chapter 4, but we would like to emphasise that they are only part of that family (see Chapters 5, 6 and 7). Further, we want to highlight that those academic skills that served well at first degree level, and even at master's level, require considerable development to enable candidates to complete a doctoral study. Let us illustrate our point with a metaphor.

In the case of swimming, our early experiences and efforts in swimming baths may well have made us strong competitors in local and even national races and, indeed, we may have won so many that we had been chosen to represent our country's team at the Olympics. We would then have had to adapt our skills to a much bigger pool and develop our techniques, strength and stamina further to cope with the much stronger competition, albeit with a coach at the ready with instructions and a warm towel while our friends and supporters cheered us on. This is the equivalent of developing our academic prowess through school, first degree and then perhaps a master's degree. If we begin our doctoral studies expecting that the task will

FIGURE 1.1 Swimming in swimming pool

FIGURE 1.2 Swimming in the sea

involve an even bigger pool with increasingly stronger competition, then we will be surprised by the complete change in environment and skills requirements that it presents. In terms of difficulties and challenges, it is more equivalent to attempting to swim the English Channel while the sense of accomplishment at the end is more about pride in your own development than in beating off competitors.

The lanes have disappeared, only the general direction of travel is indicated; the end point is well out of sight; there are unpredictable waves and currents; the deeper water contains many terrors both below the surface and on it; and the coach can only supply general guidance and encouragement over your long, drawn-out personal battle with the elements. S/he will help by alerting you to possible dangers and may guide you through the shipping lanes. Your friends and supporters wave you off from the shore and a few might make the journey to the other side to congratulate you when you reach the other shore. Otherwise you will be alone, ploughing on regardless of being weary and cold, as you learn to tolerate the mental uncertainty … and the jellyfish and other unexpected floating and swimming objects. However, there will be patches of calm water in which to recoup some energy and reflect on how far you have come; you will feel a rush of serotonin-powered elation when you realise that a sleepless night has resulted in a major move forward; your strokes will be more powerful as you progress and you will experience joy when you reach what previously appeared to be an unobtainable goal.

This is a different task with new rules, not all of which will have been clear when you volunteered for it. Although your swimming skills, competitive spirit, strong body and so on, which have served you well so far, will stand you in good stead during the rest of the journey, there will be other skills to be learnt and practised along the way. Further, not every gold medal winner from the swimming pool will excel at this new task, while some who did not make the national team will bring other skills to bear which will see them safely to the opposite shore.

We guess that you will see how this analogy applies to the process of doctoral study, with other comparisons emerging with greater experience of it. For instance, the ability to learn new things is of course important in both the swimming baths and sea, at undergraduate and postgraduate level, but the skills of discriminating, evaluating and challenging received wisdom become predominant at the doctoral level and not everyone has practised this before. What is more, those skills, while important in the academic context, may need some adaptation when encountering other work environments, as you will see in Chapters 8 and 9. Further, if the 2012 London Para-Olympics taught us nothing else, it did demonstrate that having a perfect body is not essential for swimming excellence, which resonates with our own experience that a traditional background of school and university success is not an essential precursor for the development of a good researcher. Those with a more varied background have often developed other pertinent skills along the way.

Beyond the doctorate – why learning generic, transferable skills is important

To prolong the metaphor a bit longer: armed with the experience of the English Channel, you will be better prepared to swim in other seas, some of which, some of the time, will be less demanding or will require only minor adaptations to your skill inventory. Then you will become adept at spotting the need for a new skill and acquiring it in time for ocean crossings.

In the Prologue we referred to the notion that the development of skills has always been a facet of doctoral education, but only an implicit part in the past when the prime objective was to reach the goal of producing a thesis that demonstrated the work towards, and the achievement of, an original contribution to knowledge. Of course skills were learnt in the process but, first, they tended to be mainly those developed in relation to a specific research project and, secondly, there was little encouragement to articulate them explicitly. In the past, when few people attained a doctorate and the likely career pursued thereafter was one in Higher Education, academic employers understood the requirements and outcomes of academic study and took for granted that they had been achieved by people with a doctorate seeking a research-related role in the academy. (Of course then, and occasionally now, people undertook doctoral study not for any future employment but simply as an intellectual challenge. If you are such a person, we suspect that you will find it satisfying to monitor what other skills are acquired along the way to the academic achievement, especially as many of these will be survival skills in the general game of life!)

In terms of pursuing a career beyond the doctorate, times have changed. In the next section we will review how things changed, and why, but now a larger number of people with high academic qualifications are seeking employment in a very wide range of work situations, while employers require clear articulation of how the attributes acquired during doctoral study and research work meet their needs. They prefer these attributes to be readily transferable from the doctorate/research to the work situation, whatever it is. This has led to the use of specific terms for such attributes: **generic and transferable skills**. They are defined as *generic* in that they are not restricted to a particular task or work environment and *transferable* in that, having been learnt/practised in one situation, they are flexible and can be applied to another task in another situation, albeit with some modification.

Using our example in Activity 1.1, the skill of handling difficult people, learned through vacation work or other jobs, can be transferred during doctoral study to managing supervisors or research participants and then transferred again to dealing with seniors and clients as a professional beyond the doctorate. Before we discuss the process of development of the 'skills agenda' in doctoral education, Activity 1.2 will provide you with a clearer picture of what is meant by transferable skills and may provide you with more ideas about, and examples of, some that you already have and could use to enhance your employment prospects.

ACTIVITY 1.2   UNDERSTANDING TRANSFERABILITY

Go back to your own example, or use ours of a waiter or bartender, from Activity 1.1 and list the attributes, that is qualities and skills, which make for an excellent holder of that job. Now cross out that first job title and substitute the job 'manager'. Cross out any attributes that no longer apply.

How many of them remain roughly the same across both jobs? These are transferable skills since they are useful, with a bit of adaptation, across several jobs. Since academics and researchers often have to manage people as part of their roles, they are transferable both within and outside of the academy.

This exercise is based on one by Linda Herold, Sir Sandford Fleming College, Cobourg, Ontario, www.steppingstonesforvets.org/Skills/Identifying_Our_Transferable_Skills_In_Career_Planning.pdf (retrieved 23/4/2013).

The development of skills training in the doctorate – a potted history providing the rationale

Earlier we recognised that there have recently been significant changes in doctoral education, mentioning the growth in numbers and diversity of participants, and the purpose of the doctorate. The doctorate continues to be a main entry qualification for work in the academy itself but is increasingly being used, if not always as a specified qualification, for obtaining work at a senior level across the range of sectors, public, private and voluntary, in a wide range of professions. Not only are professional people seeking to obtain a doctorate to improve their promotion chances within a specific career pathway, but also, because of qualification inflation and increasing unemployment, the doctorate is sought to indicate exceptional skill within an increasingly competitive environment. It is worth noting that, although we will illustrate here these transformations with examples from the UK context, they are happening globally.

The nature of doctoral training had changed little before 1987, being largely viewed as an apprenticeship in research, with students learning by working with an expert researcher, their supervisor, to develop a research project and a thesis in the supervisor's field (or subject area) of expertise. Such apprenticeships were often spread over many years, a source of worry to funders of research, resulting in the 1987 Winfield Report, which expressed concerns about over-long completion rates and the consequent cost of studentships. This was the first real interaction between government and universities about doctoral education and led to some disciplines in some universities developing training provision for doctoral students, mainly confined to lessons about research methods, although some provided advice on how to write a thesis and survive the doctoral journey. This is where our more detailed history begins.

Research methods programmes became more widespread across universities and disciplines within them, as many research councils (RCs) began to institute 'recognition exercises', limiting research student funding to institutions that provided such students with a good research training programme. By the 1990s, especially following the 1996 Harris Report reviewing postgraduate education, universities began to extend this training provision to all registered doctoral researchers in recognition of economies of scale, the benefits of peer group learning, quality considerations and, quite probably, publicity and recruitment advantages. Thus by the time the Bologna Declaration 1999 was published, the UK had already established methods training in its Higher Education Institutions (HEIs), and a few institutions also provided broader skills training, mainly related to research communication and dissemination. The Bologna Declaration sought to reform European Higher Education systems and produce some convergence across Europe in order to improve graduate employability, mobility and global competitiveness.

By 2010, following an onslaught of policy initiatives, as exemplified in Box 1.1, the UK HEIs had all made provision of some kind in relation to transferable skills training, many establishing Graduate Schools of some form or another or creating similar professional teams charged with postgraduate (PGR) and early career researcher (ECR) development. In more recent times, coalitions within and between universities (Doctoral Training Centres/Centres for Doctoral Training or Partnerships: DTCs, CDTs, DTPs) have been formed under research council initiatives which aim to provide excellence in research by drawing on a wider range of expertise within a context of a critical mass of researchers.

As can be seen in Box 1.1, the development of policy and intervention by government in the education and training of newer researchers increased considerably from 2000 with at least one (and frequently more) review, report or recommendation emerging per annum. You need not study these in detail now but we alert you to their significance in promoting and embedding the need for PGRs/ECRs to gain an appropriate selection of transferable skills to aid their future careers, and hence contribute to the national and continental economy.

BOX 1.1   IMPORTANT POLICY DOCUMENTS IMPACTING ON POSTGRADUATE RESEARCH EDUCATION AND EARLY CAREER RESEARCHERS

- 1987 Winfield Report, Completion rates and studentships
- 1996 Harris Report, Review of PG Education
- 1999 QAA Code of Practice, Section 1; reviewed in 2004
- 1999* Bologna Declaration plus annual revisions and additions
- 2001 and 2008 QAA Framework for HE Qualifications revised

- 2001 RCUK, Joint Statement of the Skills Training Requirements for Research Students (JSS)
- 2002 Roberts Report, *Set for Success*
- 2003 HEFCE Improving Standards in Postgraduate Research Degree Programmes
- 2003 DES Investing in Innovation
- 2004* Dublin Descriptors
- 2005* Salzburg I Principles
- 2005* European Charter for Researchers and Code of Conduct for the Recruitment of Researchers
- 2006 Leitch Review, Prosperity for all in the global economy – world-class skills
- 2006 Warry Report, *Increasing the Economic Impact of the Research Councils*
- 2008 UUK International Unit The UK's Competitive Advantage
- 2008 The Concordat to Support the Career Development of Researchers (UK)
- 2009 Thrift Review, Research Careers in the UK
- 2009 Wellings Report, universities' management of IP
- 2009 DBIS Higher Ambitions
- 2010 DBIS Review of Postgraduate education
- 2011* Salzburg II
- 2011 QAA Doctoral Degree Characteristics
- 2012 QAA Review of Section 1 Code of Practice for Research Degrees

  * European

As we are writing this book yet another document was launched at Westminster: the 2012 report of an independent inquiry on postgraduate education by the Higher Education Commission: www.policyconnect.org. uk/hec/research/postgraduate-education. Although the main substance of the review focused on the funding of and access to postgraduate studies, the Commission agreed with the findings of the 2006 Leitch Review that postgraduate skills are major drivers of innovation and growth. Further, it suggested it was critical to the future of the UK that a strategic approach was taken to maintain the current competitive advantage of high-quality PGR skills' training by strengthening the support of PGRs and increasing the UK's share of leading researchers.

The pervasiveness of professional skill development

Lest you think that this concentration on skill development is the unique province of researchers, we should note that all professions have, over the same time period, reviewed and enhanced their requirements for Continuing Professional Development. It is no coincidence that the skills highlighted for professional researchers have much in common with those expected of other professional people, underlining their transferability. To give an example, Berliner (2001: 469–70), when addressing teachers about what can be learnt from expert teachers, described what he called the prototypical features of expertise to be found in a range of professional fields. These are summarised in Box 1.2.

BOX 1.2   PROTOTYPICAL FEATURES OF EXPERTISE, SUMMARISED FROM BERLINER, D.C. (2001) LEARNING ABOUT AND LEARNING FROM EXPERT TEACHERS, *INTERNATIONAL JOURNAL OF EDUCATIONAL RESEARCH* 35 (5): 463–482

- Extensive discipline content knowledge and deep understanding
- Improved use of knowledge
- Better problem-solving strategies
- Superior skills for adaptation and improvisation
- More challenging objectives devised
- Enhanced decision making skills
- Improved ability to read cues
- Greater sensitivity to context
- Advanced monitoring and feedback skills
- More frequent hypothesis testing
- Greater respect for colleagues

Particular recent developments in skills training

From the foregoing, we can see that the apprenticeship model of research training was increasingly challenged over the last 25 years. Further, the limitations of research methods training alone became apparent during the last 15 years. In response, at least in part, to employers' requirements for their doctoral recruits to be highly skilled as well as having a high intellectual capacity, in 2001 the research councils (RCs) produced a statement on skills training requirements, or the Joint Statement Skills (JSS – see Appendix 1) as it became known, which essentially was a summary of the skills required of successful doctoral candidates by the time they submitted their theses. The JSS acted as the basis for generic research skills training programmes, tailored to the needs of individual students through Learning

Needs Analysis (sometimes called Training or Development Needs Analysis) procedures, something we will explore further in the next chapter. This development recognised that the specialist skills derived from a particular research project were no longer sufficient to meet contemporary requirements and that PGRs needed to improve their ability to recognise and articulate their skills to a wider audience other than their doctoral examiners. This generated an ongoing debate about the nature of the doctorate and the postdoctoral career.

It is common sense that no prospective employer, even one in Higher Education, is going to read a candidate's thesis to discern what skills and attributes they might bring to the world of work; instead the candidate must be able to identify and communicate their increased prowess and knowledge in a way that makes sense to employers. Further, the communication of acquired skills to gain employment must be followed by a demonstration of those skills in the new context while performing the job.

Following the recommendations in the Sir Gareth Roberts 2002 UK report *Set for Success*, funding was made available for a limited period of ten years as an incentive to institutions to establish and embed training of transferable skills in doctoral study and postdoctoral support, including those engaged in a full- or part-time mode. At the same time, supervisors/training deliverers across the sector also required development support to meet these changing circumstances. Although institutions provided some internal staff development support, the efforts of external organisations such as UKGRAD, which later became Vitae, the UK Council for Graduate Education (UKCGE), and the Society for Research in Higher Education Postgraduate Interest Group (SRHE PIN) enabled the sharing of good practice and joint consideration of challenges and potential solutions across the sector.

As the 'Roberts' funding period came to an end, the RCs began, in response to diminishing resources, to develop their funding strategy to emphasise the use and sharing of excellence in training provision through centres of excellence variously named DTCs, CDTs or DTPs, etc. At the same time the limitations of the JSS became apparent because it was recognised that skills demand continuous development over a career lifetime.

Vitae (the UK organisation that champions researcher development) responded to this by producing the Researcher Development Framework (RDF) – a process in which your authors were heavily involved. We will look at this in more detail later, but here provide Vitae's introduction:

> The Researcher Development Framework articulates the knowledge, behaviours and attributes of successful researchers and encourages them to aspire to excellence through achieving higher levels of development.

Similar initiatives have been pursued in other countries across Europe and worldwide. For instance, in Australia the second edition (2013) of the Australian Qualifications Framework (AQF) specifies, in addition to original research outcomes presented in a thesis or equivalent, that generic learning outcomes will fall into four broad categories: fundamental skills, people skills, thinking skills and personal skills or attributes (www.gradskills. anu.edu.au/). The impact that the transferable skills initiatives have had on the sector as a whole can be judged by reading the report by the Leading European Research Universities (LERU): *Doctoral degrees beyond 2010: Training talented researchers for society.* www.leru.org/files/publications/ LERU_Doctoral_degrees_beyond_2010.pdf (accessed 22/2/2013).

A flavour of this report can be gleaned from the following excerpt:

> The process of doctoral education develops in the candidate a range of skills to a very advanced level. These skills relate not only to the research process itself, but also to a broader personal and professional training and development. The latter skills are often labelled as 'generic' or 'transferable', because they are valuable not only for the successful completion of the doctorate, but also for career development after the doctorate in a wide range of professional sectors. (LERU 2010: 5)

Such radical change does not come without consequences for the people involved, a topic we turn to in the last section of this chapter.

Impact on the people involved in PGR/ECR education and training

It is not only the doctoral and postdoctoral researchers who are influenced by these far-reaching developments; their supervisors, principal investigators (PIs), Graduate School Directors, trainers, and other support staff have all had to develop their skills and change their traditional working practice in response. Indeed, it could be that the researchers themselves are the least aware of the changes since they may not realise that previously things were very different. However, they (you, perhaps) are the ones who have to make the most personal effort to engage with the changes; becoming self-aware, seeking opportunities for further development and ensuring the development of a competitive advantage when in search of further employment.

Academics may have been crusaders, champions, weary compliers or resistant to change in relation to the various policy edicts as they have constantly been asked to do more with less support (financial at least) in the last 15 years; yet the vast majority now recognise that skill development improves the quality of research produced while there is growing evidence that it does not substantially increase the registration time for doctoral students. Vitae and other related organisations hope that the RDF will help academics to identify their own training needs as well as those of their postgraduate and staff researchers.

A key point is that, no matter how personally stimulating the process of obtaining a doctorate can be, doctorates are no longer the exceptional qualifications they once were. In today's competitive job market, in addition to demonstrating autonomous learning in relation to a specific research project, holders of a doctoral qualification must convince future employers that they have become proficient researchers with broad skills which are transferable to other occupational situations. Since standing still is not an option, it is with this task that this book seeks to provide you with support to identify what further skills you might need.

Ideas for further reading

Denicolo, P.M., Park, C., Clarke, G. and Bohrer, J. *Doctorateness – An Elusive Concept?* Available online at: www.qaa.ac.uk/Publications/InformationAndGuidance/Pages/Doctorateness---an-elusive-concept.aspx (retrieved 23/4/2013).

DfES (2003) *The Future of Higher Education.* London: HMSO.

Gough, M. and Denicolo, P.M. (2007) *Research Supervisors and the Skills Agenda: Learning Needs Analysis and Personal Development Profiling.* No.1 in Series of consultative guides produced by the Postgraduate Issues Network. London: SRHE.

HEFCE (1996) *Review of Postgraduate Education (Harris Report).* Bristol: HEFCE. Available online at: www.hefce.ac.uk/pubs/hefce/1996/m14_96.htm (retrieved 23/4/2013).

Kemp, N., Archer, W., Gilligan, C. and Humpfrey, C. (2008) *The UK's Competitive Advantage: The Market for International Research Students.* London: UK Higher Education International Unit.

QAA *Quality Code for Higher Education, Chapter B11 Research Degrees.* Available online at: www.qaa.ac.uk/Publications/InformationAndGuidance/Pages/quality-code-B11.aspx (retrieved 23/4/2013).

Roberts, G. (2002) *SET for Success: The Supply of People with Science, Technology, Engineering and Mathematic Skills.* London: HMSO.

Vitae (2009) *Researcher Development Framework.* Available at Vitae website: www.vitae.ac.uk/rdf (retrieved 25/09/2013).

2

HOW CAN RESEARCHERS IDENTIFY WHICH TRANSFERABLE SKILLS ARE NEEDED?

Chapter overview

This chapter discusses:

- The terms used in different contexts for skill identification and recording
- Identification of current skills
- Decisions about the development of future skills
- The Researcher Development Planner

Multiple terms with common meanings

As we indicated in the previous chapter, the drive towards supporting PGRs and ECRs in developing their skills extended rapidly across Higher Education Institutions (HEIs) with the advent of financial support (Roberts Funding) in the UK. (Equally, the advent of high interest in 'employability' skills has spread throughout Europe, and indeed globally, in a challenging economic climate.) The policy documents which supplied the impetus, and the institutions which provided the courses and other support for skills learning, all recognised that individual researchers each brought to their further studies a unique range of skills derived from previous life experience. Therefore institutions developed their own means through which researchers could identify the skills they already possessed and those that they needed to acquire at specific points in their journey towards, initially, achieving a doctorate. As with many other common concepts and processes in Higher Education, this skills identification activity was labelled in a variety of ways both within and between institutions.

The simplest label, derived from industrial and business settings and linked explicitly with the need for institutions to present some training courses, was Training Needs Analysis (TNA). TNA was (and still is) commonplace in the corporate sector but for some academics the word 'training' felt rather at odds with their perception that the purpose of academe is to educate. They recognised that certain skills, such as those listed in the Joint Skills Statement (JSS) for example (see Appendix 1), were in the main intellectual skills (such as constructing argument and understanding issues), not simply mechanical, performance-related skills, so some institutions adopted the label Learning Needs Analysis (LNA). Yet other perspectives focused on the purpose of developing the personal and professional skills of researchers and so preferred the label Development Needs Analysis (DNA). What these have in common is that they are all useful tools for both individuals and organisations to: mark an individual's starting point (what is sometimes called 'benchmarking'), identify what is needed to help them move forward (that is, become a better researcher), and provide the means for monitoring their progress. The format of each of these tools will be determined by the purpose of the organisation or institution.

This is more than a moot point; the aim will determine what kind of measurements need to be made of a person and, beyond this, which changes or interventions should be made or are needed. So, for example, if they wanted to create a more enterprising or entrepreneurial researcher (that is, one who could work collaboratively with industry or could set up their own business) they would need to decide what factors and/or characteristics distinguish a successful entrepreneurial researcher and then measure/analyse candidates against them. Perhaps they might find that they need practice in communicating with companies in business rather than academic language, or they may need some entirely new characteristics, for example, a good working knowledge of Intellectual Property Rights or how to establish a patent. The next step would be to provide a programme to develop these skills with mechanisms to monitor and review their progress; they might even assess the impact of such programmes and calculate the financial return on investing in such researchers! See Appendix 2 for a diagrammatic overview of the development cycle.

Having said this, it is quite likely that this relationship between people, aims and processes will not be as coherent or explicitly stated within HEIs as it is in the corporate sector (although this situation is changing). This does not mean that HEIs do not have agreed expectations about how their researchers should develop (because they clearly do, as demonstrated by doctoral up-grade/confirmation processes, research staff promotions and annual progress reviews for both), but we recognise that the formal steps mentioned above may not be overtly in place in every part of all HEIs.

However, certain disciplines have for many years had professional frameworks that determine skill requirements, for example nursing, teaching, pharmacy and psychology; further, in the UK, the funding bodies have issued statements of expectation regarding the standard of training for doctoral researchers (originally invoking the JSS and, more recently, the extended framework created to cover the full spectrum of research careers, that is the Researcher Development Framework (RDF) discussed below).

An organisation (such as an HEI, professional body, research funding body, research team or department) could decide to measure or analyse any number of things, including a researcher's:

- Existing knowledge
- Skills and abilities
- Experience
- Behaviour
- Attitude and aptitude
- Moral qualities and personal integrity
- Strengths
- Weaknesses, gaps or deficits in any of the above
- Performance (as an individual researcher and/or in a specific role)
- Team performance (individual contribution to the team's performance)
- Improvement over time in subject knowledge, skill, behaviour, attitude, integrity, performance

Your organisation might want to measure or analyse your skill, your competence or your development (see Glossary for clarification of these terms) in these areas. The possibilities for variation are considerable: for example, they might be looking for gaps or deficits in your knowledge or skills which they would then aim to remedy; they might be keen to identify your strengths so that they could make better use of them; conversely, they might identify your weaknesses to make sure they did not give you a task you could not do; or they might be seeking to develop you to take up a role or task in the future (this last frequently comes under the remit of 'talent management'). The method they might use (as with all research) will vary with what they want to measure. Common methods include:

- Interviews
- Surveys and questionnaires
- Observation
- Detailed job and/or task analysis
- Skills matrices
- Appraisal systems, which may include a '360 degree' appraisal (see Glossary)

In Higher Education you are most likely to encounter the skills matrix method of analysis, for example in the TNA, DNA, LNA, skills audits discussed above, although development centres involving observation and task/job analysis derived originally from industry are also being used. The skills audit approaches recognise that the learning and development of transferable skills at the doctoral level have cognitive and affective (intellectual and emotional) components, and appreciate that these will require further refinement and professional tuning at the postdoctoral level.

Whichever of this range of terms is prevalent in your own research environment, the intention is the same: to compare current knowledge, ability and approach to that required for the completion of a specific programme of study (say, a doctoral degree) or to reach a required standard within a profession or role (now that we can consider the whole research career using the RDF). This produces a tailored approach that explicitly recognises the diversity of researchers, and provides a first step in helping you aspire to improve on attributes appropriate to your developing researcher role. It is important to recognise that each of us brings a range of abilities and knowledge to the research projects we work on and we will all have differing development needs related to our aspirations for the future. A range of possible aspirations is provided in Box 2.1 for you to reflect on to identify your own current ones.

BOX 2.1   RANGE OF POSSIBLE ASPIRATIONS

Aspirations related to:

Personal goals: related to the kind of researcher you want to be and the professional career path you envisage taking;

Specific project: the knowledge and skills you need to acquire to implement it and the attitudes and abilities you will need to complete a specific, challenging task;

Organisational objectives: set by the degree awarding institution and perhaps by professional bodies or future employers in your field.

These in turn may be:

Immediate: related to your current project;

Requiring time: for instance, the building of an international reputation;

Clear from documents: usually from the professional bodies or found in job descriptions;

Subject to change with experience: often those in the first group, the personal ones;

Needing guidance from experts in the field and your level of study, usually your supervisors or principal investigator (PI) (particularly those related to your current project), or from careers experts.

We will consider the wide range of skills that might be embedded in such aspirations in more detail in Chapters 4, 5, 6 and 7, but first let us focus on the skills that you already have.

Identification of current skills

In the previous chapter we suggested that you already possess a range of transferable skills and you might like to keep that list to hand as you read on here about how you might approach your first meeting with your supervisor or PI (or indeed any other appraisal or review meeting). Even if you are already well embarked on your current project you might find it useful to check back on the CV and accompanying documents (application) that you provided when applying for your current post. In compiling that application you had to identify the knowledge and those skills and abilities that would make you a good candidate for the post and you probably had to supply some evidence to support your contentions, either as documents or during interviews. This means that you can have some confidence now in recognising that you already have some generic skills that have transferred from your previous education and other experience into doctoral education or beyond (see Chapter 1). You might like to confirm this by undertaking the exercise in Activity 2.1.

ACTIVITY 2.1   IDENTIFYING MATCHES BETWEEN ORIGINAL APPLICATION AND SOME KEY SKILLS

We have drawn these skills from the Joint Skills Statement (JSS) list for simplicity since they are incorporated in the more extensive and detailed Researcher Development Framework (RDF) discussed later.

First, review your application documents highlighting those areas of knowledge, abilities and personal attributes that you claimed to have. You might find it helpful to list them using the JSS headings down the side of a table and the headings Skills, Knowledge and Experience across the top:

Research skills and techniques (gained from previous research projects at undergraduate or master's level, but also from personal research such as evaluating a choice of purchases);

Understanding and appreciation of the research environment (again drawn from previous studies but also from such things as being aware of health and safety in a work environment and any background exploration you made about research practice prior to applying for your current role);

Research management (here your literature searching skills might be applicable but also any activity in which you had to plan, prioritise and achieve milestones will have developed some organisation skills);

Personal effectiveness (you have certainly already demonstrated a willingness to learn but consider when you might have demonstrated creativity, flexibility, self-awareness, recognition of boundaries, and self-discipline);

Communication skills (you will certainly have had experience in writing in an academic format, though perhaps not in the specific style required at this higher level, and you may already have experience of public speaking);

Networking and team working (do not neglect your experience in sports, leisure or voluntary groups as well as that from previous work situations);

Career management (you have definitely made several steps in career management to get where you are now – the foundation for your future!)

Now you can compare your list to the full JSS in Appendix 1 so that you identify where you already have a skill, at least in embryonic form. Next, be brave and identify the gaps – the areas that you need to work on more.

After completing Activity 2.1 you will have a good basis on which to conduct effective discussions with your supervisor/PI about what you need to begin to develop, or develop further, and what might be the preferred order of working on these attributes to fit with the requirements of your project. Preparing in this way for this kind of meeting has another benefit beyond giving some degree of self-confidence – it demonstrates that you are maturing as an autonomous learner, taking some responsibility for your own professional development.

You can enhance that impression by also considering, and researching, a range of possible ways in which you can develop your skills profile and build your professional portfolio (we will have more to say on portfolios in Chapter 8). We will consider and make suggestions about your profile in the next section but first we want you to explore what support is provided in your own institution to help you construct your current profile and identify any gaps. Each institution is likely to have some form of skills identification system since the Quality Assurance Agency, in its Code of Practice for Postgraduate Researchers (www.qaa.ac.uk/Publications/InformationAndGuidance/Pages/quality-code-B11.aspx), contains guidance to institutions about providing opportunities for researchers to identify, work on and review their development needs. Similarly, the research councils expect that institutions will have in place mechanisms for monitoring, evaluating and improving researcher skills.

Such systems usually include a matrix, similar to that in Box 2.2 for PGRs, which lists skills, what they look like in practice, ratings that indicate current ability and space for ratings at a later stage, say at fixed points in the degree process or after training or research experience. Some include a column in which sources of evidence for skill acquisition can be logged, and others list means by which an initial level of skill can be developed. Producing evidence of your skills is essential for proving that you have engaged in a developmental activity of some kind and for demonstrating your prowess. This system enables an individual to audit their skills and compile a Personal Development Plan (PDP), discussed further in Chapter 8, while at the same time identifying learning needs.

BOX 2.2   SAMPLE EXTRACT FROM A GRADUATE RESOURCE BOOK – DEVELOPMENT NEEDS ANALYSIS SECTION – PROVIDED BY KIND PERMISSION OF UNIVERSITY OF MANCHESTER (2006)

Skill Level ratings: 1 = good first degree graduate standard; 2 = a PhD student with some experience; 3 = an experienced PhD student; 4 = a particularly able PhD student

Research Skills and Techniques To be Able to Demonstrate: (from section A of JSS)	Characteristic descriptor (level 3 – an experienced student)	Initial Competence Level	Year 1 Competence Level	Example of Possible Evidence	Training Courses Supporting Development in the Area
[....]		1 2 3 4	1 2 3 4		
2. Original, independent and critical thinking, and the ability to develop theoretical concepts	Able to formulate hypotheses and/or research questions for the purposes of designing a personal research project. Able to provide new and innovative research ideas. Able to objectively and knowledgeably criticise published research.	1 2 3 4	1 2 3 4	Patent application	Introductory Course: Critical Thinking Seminar

---

| 3. A knowledge of recent advances within one's field and in related areas | Can communicate knowledgeably about their research topic with supervisor and peers, debating concepts. Familiar with the relevant literature. Can write a literature review of publication standard on the topic. | 1 2 3 4 | 1 2 3 4 | Supervisor feedback on progress report. Lit. review | Introductory Course: Academic writing workshop; library training |
| [...] | | 1 2 3 4 | 1 2 3 4 | | |

The example given in Box 2.2 provides a good illustration of how the skills listed in the JSS were being used and elaborated on so that doctoral researchers and supervisors could be clear about how they manifest themselves in practice. Gradually, there also emerged a desire to extend the JSS idea beyond the end of the doctorate to enable people to develop a profile of their skills at any stage of a research career and, most significantly, to see what higher levels of skill they could aspire to gain. Added to this, there was increasing recognition of the importance of building research capacity by developing highly skilled researchers while promoting the role of researcher as a valued profession within a competitive global market.

The seeds were thus sown for an overarching competency model of professional learning built on the JSS, resulting in the Researcher Development Framework (RDF) and the Researcher Development Statement (RDS), now the key reference document for policy and strategy development in relation to postgraduate researchers' skills and attributes and those of researchers employed in Higher Education in the UK and increasingly in Europe and abroad.

The RDF was launched in 2011 and has been adopted by most UK HEIs for use by individual researchers and those who support them and is included in research councils' doctoral training provision. The RDS has been incorporated in the QAA Quality Code Section B11, the section on research degrees, and complements Principles 3 and 4 of the *Concordat to Support the Career Development of Researchers* (which contains the European

Charter for Researchers and *Code of Conduct for the Recruitment of Researchers*). The full RDF and RDS and other useful related documents can be found on the Vitae website: www.vitae.ac.uk/methodology.

You might like to engage in Activity 2.2, a process similar to that which generated the attributes/skills list for the RDF.

ACTIVITY 2.2   ATTRIBUTES OF A GOOD RESEARCHER

Giving yourself a few minutes, list the main attributes that you think describe a good researcher. Compare your list with that in the summary version of the RDF, presented in the form of a wheel (with the central four domains, 12 sub-domains and 63 descriptors) in Appendix 3.

Throughout the book we will note some of the most common ones elicited from experienced researchers, with which you can compare your answers.

The full RDF and RDS and other useful, related, documents can be found on the postgraduate researchers or the research staff sections of the Vitae website: www.vitae.ac.uk.

What you might find helpful about the RDF is that the skills (originally identified by experienced, practising researchers) are presented as attributes or descriptors in the full document, arranged in a matrix to show how they develop over time. The matrix lists the descriptors relevant to each of the domains in the vertical axis while the horizontal axis displays them as they present themselves over five phases of career development, the first two phases being of particular relevance to PGRs/ECRs. However, do not feel restricted by this. You might aspire to develop some skills beyond phase two if you already have reached that level during earlier research or professional practice.

If the RDF is new to you, then you might feel overwhelmed by it at first sight because there seem to be so many skills involved in the role of researcher. While the JSS presented a summary of skill requirements, the RDF goes into much finer detail about the attributes required of a researcher. Do not let this put you off exploring it further: keep in mind that you have chosen a very skilled profession and that already you have some of these skills in embryonic form at least. One benefit of such detail is that it gives you a better sense of what the attribute looks like when it is present. This makes it easier to identify for yourself or for others whether you have reached a particular phase. Further, the objective is not to develop all the attributes at once. You must make some decisions about what is relevant to develop and in what order as you continue to pursue your career, but we usually recommend that researchers select from three to five attributes to develop per annum. While the RDF can help you to easily identify your current attributes, discerning your future needs requires additional expertise as well as effort.

Deciding on the development of future skills

We suggested earlier that, having made a first attempt at identifying for yourself what skills you may already have and some of the gaps that seem to be apparent, you should share your results with your supervisor or PI. There are three very good reasons for this, which we present in Box 2.3.

BOX 2.3   REASONS FOR DISCUSSING WITH YOUR SUPERVISOR/PI OR MENTOR YOUR PERSONAL SKILLS DEVELOPMENT PROGRAMME

1. Procedural reason: most supervisors/PIs are likely to expect, and be expected by the organisation, to help you with your analysis of current skills and other attributes and the process of developing them further. Most HEIs now will also be required to evaluate your progress in acquiring them – we will discuss this in Chapter 8. However, it is worth noting that although most universities in the UK, and a growing number in Europe, refer to the RDF when devising and monitoring their researcher training provision, not all do. Further, not all supervisors and PIs are familiar with its detail. We discuss how you might approach this matter at the beginning of Chapter 3.
2. Discipline reason: although the attributes in the RDF are intended to be generic, it is recognised that there will be differences in fine detail across disciplines.
3. Project reason: the actual project that you are embarked on will require specific skills and attributes at different stages and your supervisors/PIs will give you an insight into which ones to prioritise at each stage.

Let us provide you with an example. All research projects (except those using a pure grounded theory approach) require that, before you finally decide on the research hypothesis or question, you examine the literature to find out what research has already been conducted, by what methods and with what result, in that area. Aha, you may be thinking, I know how to do that – I have done a literature search before. That is a good start, but are you familiar with the library layout and bibliographic retrieval systems, including the virtual layout and systems, in your current library? If not, then that is the first learning step. Having identified and retrieved a selection of relevant material and then read it, you may (if you are a doctoral researcher, for example) then prepare a review to show to your supervisor. In our roles as student advisors we frequently hear newer researchers saying that their literature review is considered by their supervisor/PI to be too descriptive, not analytical and critical enough. Indeed, being able to provide an appropriately critical discussion becomes one of the most frequently sought-after research skills. Thus, it may be a good one to include in your list of skills to acquire fairly rapidly. In contrast, you may notice references in the library literature to other attributes, such as becoming familiar with different modes of dissemination – but this can wait a while until you are approaching the point of having something to disseminate.

As well as seeking the support of your senior colleagues, there is now another tool to help you with the task of identifying your future needs. In 2012 Vitae developed a Researcher Development Planner, a web-based application to guide researchers in identifying their expertise, capabilities and further development. This is discussed in the final section of this chapter, which has been provided by Ellen Pearce, the Director of Vitae.

The Researcher Development Framework Planner

The RDF has been developed into an online planner in response to calls from universities and researchers. It enables you to reflect on your capabilities and experience, record evidence against the various descriptors and levels, and prioritise and plan your future professional development.

There are many ways to use the RDF Planner, depending on your own preferences and style. It can be useful to consider what kind of timeframe you want to work with before starting to record objectives and actions. For some, reviewing the plan on a monthly basis is a useful regular check which helps to keep focus on key areas, while some researchers prefer to review their own progress and plans yearly or as part of annual review meetings with their supervisor or PI, and for more experienced researchers a five- or even a ten-year vision that includes interim actions and objectives works well.

You also need to consider how best to use such a comprehensive framework. For some, systematically working through the whole framework, from knowledge and intellectual abilities, personal effectiveness, research governance and organisation to engagement, influence and impact, is the most useful approach. However, you may want to prioritise key areas on which to focus. For example, if you are new to research, you might focus first on domain A, which covers research methods and subject knowledge, the cognitive abilities for undertaking research, and creativity and intellectual insight. If you are further through your research career, focusing on Domain D might feel more appropriate as it emphasises the wider impact of research.

Vitae have also distilled a series of 'lenses' which filter the aspects of the RDF according to a particular theme. So, for example, if you are interested in developing your leadership potential, you can highlight the particular aspects of the RDF that are relevant. (A new function of the tool is currently being developed that allows filtering by lenses – this may be available by the time you read this.)

Once you have decided on your approach, you can use the tool to assess your current level for the descriptors on which you want to focus. For each individual descriptor, there are up to five development phases. As was noted earlier in the chapter, your profile over the descriptors will depend on your experiences in your current role, in other roles, from previous employment and positions you hold outside research. Generally speaking, phases move from an individual focus at phase 1, through leading teams and developing others, to working at national or international focus at phase 5. You should self-assess where you currently think you are within the five phases. If you have evidence to support this, you can upload it and link to it so you have it for future reference.

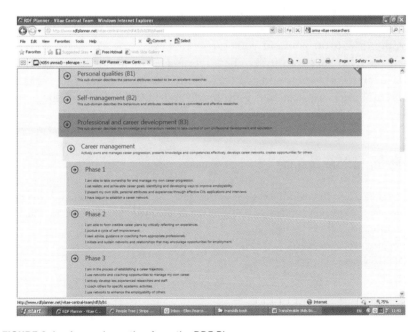

FIGURE 2.1 A sample section from the RDF Planner

Next, you can consider which of the phases you are aiming to reach, and in what timeframe. You might find it useful to talk to friends, peers, your supervisor, PI or manager, or other colleagues during the process. It can be helpful to get a sense of other people's views of your current levels of competence against the descriptors and a sense of whether they think your aims are both realistic and aspirational. (By aspirational, we mean that you should be ambitious, setting yourself targets for improvement.) But the important thing is that the plans work for, and inspire, you. For example, if you are making a three-year plan, you might want to break down the actions and you might want to specify a progression through the individual phases by various deadlines. If you are planning for six months to a year, it might be easier to specify some immediate actions to take. It can also be useful to discuss and commit to doing the actions with a friend or peer. Speaking your intention to someone else can help it stay 'alive' amidst the pressures of research and other commitments!

There are a range of links from the planner to training opportunities and resources to help you to develop each particular aspect. There are links to Vitae resources and there may also be links to your institution's training and development programmes if your institution is using this planner to support researchers. If so, they might have specific ways that they would like you to use it. For example, you might be asked to do a Development Needs Analysis during the early part of your doctorate, which you discuss with your supervisor, or it might form the basis of career development conversations with your PI at set times throughout the year or research process.

The important thing, though, is that you use the tool as a framework to provide a focus on you and your career in a way that works for you. It is based on what successful researchers themselves identified as being key to their success, and these resonate both with researchers around the world and with employers of researchers both inside and outside Higher Education.

Ideas for further reading

Most Training/Development Needs Analysis literature is written for developers, but there are examples of 'how to identify your own needs' on the internet and you may find the following useful:

Donovan, P. and Townsend, J. (2004) *Training Needs Analysis Pocketbook*. Arlesford, UK: Management Pocketbooks Ltd.

3

HOW CAN TRANSFERABLE SKILLS BE ACQUIRED?

Chapter overview

This chapter discusses:

- Negotiating expectations
- Making the most of opportunities
- Individual learning styles
- Traditional forms of learning

  - Courses and workshops
  - Reading

- Skills learnt in process of doing research
- Skills that can be learnt through other roles in the institution
- Skills that can be learnt outside the institution
- Keeping motivated

Negotiating expectations

Previously, in Box 2.3, we suggested that you should discuss your development plans with your supervisor/PI/mentor to obtain guidance about skills related to your project that will have a priority in the near and more distant future. We also alluded earlier to the small possibility that such persons may not be aware of, or convinced by, the recent emphasis on the skills agenda, for a variety of reasons. However, most of you will be fortunate enough to have a supportive, knowledgeable, senior colleague concerned to help you make the best of the current situation and prepare for the future. Whichever situation you are in, what is important is that you recognise that you are intended to be an autonomous learner, taking responsibility for your own development.

That may have seemed either a rather pompous statement or a rather scary one, depending on your current mood, your prior experience and your view of future prospects. Our response is that we too have had periods full of self-confidence, punctuated by others in which self-doubt predominated, which continue even into our mature years (exacerbated by a tendency on both our parts to bite off more than we can easily chew). We are (uncomfortably) aware of our own foibles – a skill that all researchers could benefit from cultivating. Thus we used the heading 'negotiating expectations' to incorporate the notions that you need both to discuss with your senior colleague the development of your research skills and to convince yourself of what must be done and what you are capable of doing. Other factors to consider include what you fancy doing and what you fear doing, what you will find easy to accomplish and what might be more challenging.

Having weighed together the results of all these 'negotiations', you must make your decisions about what skills to prioritise now, explore the means of acquiring them, and take action to obtain them. We elaborate on ideas to support your negotiations and how to acquire skills and develop attributes in this and following chapters.

Making the most of opportunities

There are two (at least) schools of thought about the acquisition of skills in the early years of research. The first suggests that you should grasp every possible opportunity to enhance your skill level and repertoire, on the grounds that you never know when it might come in useful. If you are based in a large research institution, training opportunities will abound, so you could fill every waking moment extending your skills inventory. Alternatively, a more utilitarian, measured approach recommends developing skills as they become needed because, if you do not have opportunity to practise them, you will forget them anyway. Like us, you may have experienced being shown how to use some wickedly clever computer function but then find, only needing it infrequently and having forgotten important parts of the process, more time has to be spent retrieving it by trial and error. Nevertheless, we are sorely tempted to advocate the taking of opportunities as they arise for several additional reasons:

1. You never know when they will arise again;
2. They are more profuse and cheaper when you are registered for a higher degree or when engaged in postdoctorate research;
3. They will add to your curriculum vitae (CV) for your next role;
4. Your current sponsors may be impressed by your dedication to learning.

On the other hand, we recognise that there are other cogent reasons for adopting a more functional approach:

1. Completing the current research project must have top priority;
2. Timely completion will impress your sponsors and add considerably to your reputation and profile;
3. All work and no play can drain your motivation (see final section of this chapter).

Therefore we counsel you to formulate a plan that focuses on what must be done and at what stage in your research while carefully weighing up each opportunity as it arises, evaluating its benefits for the present and future. Consider what it might add to your profile, at what cost in time and effort. Take advice from others but mediate it with self-knowledge. We each respond differently to pressure. Some of us relish the challenge of having lots to do; others prefer to feel well in control by engaging with the 'must do' tasks and adding the 'nice to do' tasks only as time allows. This is not the only way in which we differ in relation to learning.

Individual learning styles

We have to resist the temptation here to indulge our interest in individual difference by bombarding you with lots of detailed information regarding the many theories about learning styles, along with their tests, with which to identify your own particular variation. When you have a few spare moments (or hours if you have a predilection for self-analysis) you need only type 'learning styles' into your search engine to find a whole gamut for yourself. Instead, we remind you that we each have learning style preferences. It is useful to recognise your own, not simply to indulge that preference, but rather to encourage you to use that self-knowledge effectively and also to extend your range. We have, however, provided an overview of some alternative ways of learning in Box 3.1, presented as a selection of dimensions and as preferences for certain learning media.

BOX 3.1   SOME ALTERNATIVE WAYS OF LEARNING

Serialist or wholist approach (incremental, working step by step to build up understanding or getting an overview first and then begin to make sense of the various parts).

Superficial or deep approach (learning by heart or trying to understand meanings).

Active or passive (learning by doing, problem-solving or by listening/observing others demonstrating).

Reactive or proactive (learning as a response to need or deliberately choosing to learn, whether or not immediately necessary).

Social or solitary.

Practice in a safe, structured environment or practice in a challenging, unpredictable one.

Through:

Visual material (diagrams, pictures);

Aural (by listening, face to face or remotely);

Verbal (through the written word, lists of instructions);

Physical engagement (by doing, through practice);

Theoretical means (by working out connections and meaning, through logical reflection).

These are only a selection of the possible ways that people learn and there is no one best way. Some learning tasks benefit from particular learning modes, for instance rote learning of times tables comes in handy for rapid mental calculations but understanding numbers is useful for dealing with complex numerical data; learning to drive a car can be aided initially by observing others do so or by learning how each part works in theory, then practising elements of it, but eventually practice of the whole set of skills is required to become competent in the unpredictable environment of real roads and traffic. To come nearer to the skills required of a researcher, you may find that you prefer to learn how to use a piece of technical equipment by reading the instruction booklet, or you may learn more readily by watching someone else using it, or even, depending on the robustness and cost of the equipment and its output, by trial and error. Most people benefit from learning to present in public through pilot runs with close colleagues in a safe environment; a few need the adrenalin rush of a more risky environment of a more critical audience. You might consider now what your own learning style is by addressing the ideas in Activity 3.1.

ACTIVITY 3.1   REFLECTING ON YOUR OWN LEARNING PREFERENCES

Think back through your own, by now lengthy, learning experience. Identify a few occasions when you felt that you had really learnt something. Make some notes about the context – what happened, what you did, and what was the result. Do the same for some occasions when you found it difficult to learn. *(Examples to stimulate ideas: one of us loves a challenge and learnt not just the main essence of the periodic table but a lot of chemistry besides when presented with a lot of chemical elements, a series of practical tests to use on them and the problem of sorting them into some sort of order, but thought she would die of boredom and would never learn how to fix a recurrent computer problem when listening over the telephone to step-by-step instructions that seemed to have no logical links or meaning.)*

Are you able to identify your own learning preferences (or ours in the above example)? Can you discern a preference for a dominant learning style or do you have a large repertoire? Next time you are in a learning situation and you hear yourself think, 'I'm really enjoying this', take note of its characteristics and try to put them to use for future learning. In contrast, when you notice the characteristics that undermine your learning, seek to reduce them in future situations.

Becoming familiar with your own learning preferences will help you to select those opportunities most likely to benefit the development of your skill profile, though we also urge you to experiment with some alternative forms to make yourself more versatile and able to take advantage of a greater range of learning circumstances. For instance, if there is an option of a lecture or a hands-on workshop, choose the one that, initially, suits your style. If listening to others is not top of your list, try taking notes even if there are hand-outs. If you prefer working on your own, try sometimes to work in a small group, perhaps initially online, so you can switch off, claiming computer problems, if it gets too much or arrange a face-to-face meeting if it proves stimulating. Flexibility is a key attribute of a successful researcher while the range of learning opportunities is eclectic. We urge you to be selective, but make the best of such opportunities over the next few years.

Whatever your learning preferences, it is important to consider the advice given by Kolb in his 1984 experiential learning cycle (see Ideas for further reading) which suggests a cyclical process as in Figure 3.1. Although you can begin at any point in the cycle, for learning to occur you need to complete the whole cycle.

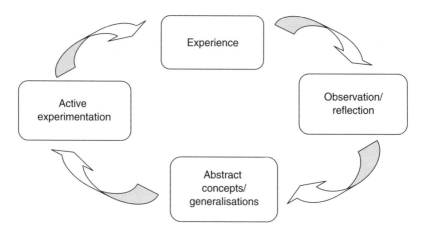

FIGURE 3.1 Kolb's learning cycle

Traditional forms of learning

By now you will be very familiar with the style of degree courses provided by HEIs but you may be less familiar with the menu of formal training programmes and workshops provided for researchers. These range from induction and discipline-specific activities arranged within your department, school or faculty, to programmes that are generic for all or most researchers, provided, again, either at faculty or university level or by specialist units such as the library, statistical centre, staff development unit, IT services. The providers might be named Graduate School, Researcher Development/Training Centre, DTC/CDT/DTP, or Centre for Staff Training and Development, and so on. It will be a good first step to get to know just what is available in your own institution and also if there are any inter-institutional opportunities for skills learning.

Do not stop looking once you have found one source for there are likely to be several formal resources for learning. For instance, the Economic and Social Research Council (ESRC) supports Doctoral Training Centres (DTCs) that may be composed of discipline strands or pathways from one or more institutions, so that doctoral researchers can attend training in their own discipline within or between institutions, or cross-disciplinary training in their own or other institutions, or avail themselves of training in advanced methods and skills through the National Centre for Research Methods (NCRM). Some ESRC DTCs also have links with other institutions that share access to advanced training and other research resources. Other research councils, learned societies and sponsors also provide for a range of training opportunities.

Such training is usually seen as an introduction to a particular skill, perhaps sometimes also providing opportunities for safe practice, but there is an expectation that participants will follow up such sessions with further reading and practice.

As a PGR or ECR you will be familiar with the need to read the relevant literature to find out about the history and current state of your discipline and particular interest area; similarly, there is a wealth of literature for transferable skills and we will suggest some books and websites that we, our colleagues and students have found useful, as we progress through this book. For those of you who like to understand the theory behind practice, need ideas to stimulate your practice or want to extend your repertoire, these resources can be helpful; they will also reassure you that others are also learning these skills.

Since we often organise and present skills workshops and, indeed, write books such as this on various skills development issues, we offer suggestions as starting points and/or reminder resources. We also recommend face-to-face learning environments for finding peers who might be prepared to give you, through a reciprocal arrangement, supportive feedback on your practice attempts or even form study/network groups/action learning sets with you. These 'struggling others' will one day form the core of your research network who will be valuable to you even when you are an ancient professor. Take it from one who knows and also see Chapter 6 for networking and Chapter 7 on collaborative working. Both of the aforementioned can be extended by engaging in non-research-related activities which provide for the development of skills that can be transferred back into research. We will address those in a moment, but first let us consider what skills you can learn during the actual process of doing research.

Skills learnt in the process of doing research

Technical and literary skills

Whatever your discipline, there will be technical and literary skills to be learnt as you progress through your research. Every researcher will need fairly advanced IT skills either for all of, or combinations of, reviewing literature, collecting data, data analysis and presentation through PowerPoint, Prezi, interactive whiteboards or other written forms. As tools to do these things become more varied, we urge you to check on how to acquire the most up-to-date methods and to find out how they are supported through your IT services, library, research centre, Graduate School, etc. A little reflection from one of us: if she had had tools such as email, Track Changes and an electronic reference organiser when she started her research career, instead of carrier pigeon and quill pen, she would have saved over her career at least an accumulated 12 months worth of tedious work which could have been spent swimming in the Caribbean, or writing another book. There will similarly be new tools in production as you read this that will speed your current and future research too. Do not let them pass you by.

The actual writing of a thesis is a unique enterprise that is seldom repeated but will provide you with a range of literary skills for writing about your research or other work in the future. In many ways it is the equivalent of a craftperson's masterpiece – a piece of work that demonstrates in miniature all the skills required of the craft and that acts as the qualification to join the guild. A thesis is intended to include evidence that you are competent to engage in many forms of research and scholarship in the future. Thus you will learn through the crafting of your thesis, with feedback from your various advisors, the skills of presenting complex ideas to an audience that is intellectually astute but not necessarily expert in your topic area, compelling them with your arguments and convincing them of the quality and relevance of your research (see Chapter 4). You will also learn, through advisory and practice workshops and then by actually giving presentations and writing articles (see Chapters 5 and 6), to offer your research in a range of modes to a wider variety of audience. Once beyond the doctorate, there will be other ways in which those skills can be transferred, and perhaps transformed, to fit other audiences, such as potential project funders, employers and collaborative colleagues.

Among these skills will be the development of personal attributes such as a disciplined approach to work and good time management. Further, there will be opportunities to learn how to become proficient in the use of equipment/kit and instruments that you will use to collect data now and perhaps in the future. Even if the same instruments are not involved in later work, your dexterity will have improved along with your understanding of the various benefits and drawbacks of different means of data or information collection. You will also learn data management techniques that will stand you in good stead in your future career (see Chapter 4).

Interpersonal skills

Again, it is hard to imagine a form of research that will not involve you in interacting in some way with other people, beyond your supervisors/advisors. In the laboratory you will be part of a research team and will interact with colleagues and technicians; in documentary research in a museum or library you must negotiate access and facilities with 'gate-keepers' of one kind or another; in social science, psychology and medical research you may work with participants who will, through your skills, provide your data. All of you will need to engage with other important 'holders of keys', from the assistants of important respondents to the administrators who provide access, or not, to various resources, as well as librarians and technical experts. In disseminating your work and seeking support for more, you will meet other participants and audiences.

Each of these others will have a different level of knowledge and skills about research in general and yours in particular, a different level of initial interest in it and be more or less willing to listen to you or engage with your project or ideas. It is not possible to be both a researcher and a hermit so continuing to develop your interpersonal skills with a research focus is a necessity. These skills are certainly extremely difficult to acquire from reading a book or from a lecture, as we shall see in Chapter 7 (though, in attending a lecture, at least you will be able to observe the local etiquette traditions – the way to ask questions, arrive and depart, indicate attention, and so on.) Books on local culture and habits will be useful at a general level if your research takes you into very different cultural environments, but the main learning modes will be observation, including listening, and practice emulation.

Such observation should be extended to all the venues in which research activities are conducted, no matter how experienced you are, because each 'micro-ecosystem' has its own system of what is considered good manners, professional behaviour, and research etiquette. You will recognise the phenomena through any experience you have had with electronic social networks in which there are expectations, some declared as rules but others more implicit, about topics and styles of discourse and taboos. Use your observational skills, find a few role models who seem to fit in well and adopt a similar style. Next, find a congenial senior colleague to take you under their wing, confessing that you would appreciate learning 'how things are done around here'. It is better to appear a little dependent than upset everyone's sensibilities by doing the wrong thing at the wrong time! The same will apply to attending conferences – if you are a newcomer to the association, then you will need to learn the rules of interaction through reading the literature, judging the tone, what is said and not said, and then observing others' interactions, listening to interactions and making friends with a regular attendee or two.

Making friends within your own institution is important too but do not restrict them to people in your own discipline. Much can be learnt about accessing facilities and resources across the institution – perhaps a piece of equipment that you could borrow to work on for an hour, a seminar that intersects with your field or demonstrates a method useful to your research. Sharing skills and knowledge with peers is useful too. Recently, a group of researchers from several disciplines shared a study office in one of our universities. The native English speakers helped the international researchers correct their written work; the typography researcher helped the others to format their theses; they practised their conference presentations together; books on skills and methods were shared; each provided a responsive audience to the others' efforts to explain their work in lay terms; the Chinese researcher provided tasty suppers, the French researcher brought back wine and the Belgian researcher offered chocolate from home visits. They have all remained friends after graduation. So you can see that there are lots of advantages to working with your peers, which also provide a foundation for future networks.

More about the development of interpersonal skills can be found in Chapter 7.

Skills learnt through other roles in the institution

Some funders of doctoral research, and some disciplines in some institutions, expect that research students will contribute a little time per week to acting as a lab demonstrator or a course tutor or a seminar organiser and leader. If this is the case for you, then value this opportunity to learn teaching skills that will add to your profile and enhance all your presentation skills. You will find much guidance for such tasks in our Series book, *Success in Research: Teaching in Higher Education*. Should you not have this obligation, either as an ECR or PGR, then volunteer your services for occasional or regular short slots. It is said that you never really understand something until you have to teach it, while there are a number of facets to providing a useful lesson or guiding another's practice that will contribute to your profile, including: organisation and planning; devising alternative ways of presenting ideas; working with different levels of expertise; presenting to small and large groups; dealing with questions.

Other roles that you could take on that would contribute to those and other skills include:

- organising seminars, discipline or methods interest groups with peers;
- representing your peers on committees both internally and externally;
- acting as a guide or 'buddy' to potential new recruits on open days.

There may be possibilities, such as temporary clerical posts, which would put you in touch with a new group of people and activities. Some universities have either an office-based and/or electronic listing of such opportunities but, if not, why not start one up? This would develop your organisational and office skills as well as extending your networks.

Skills learnt outside the institution

Increasingly, funders of doctoral research, especially those funding through some form of 'centre of excellence' in training, advocate and encourage researchers to engage in job placements or internships for short periods (up to a few months) in order to gain employment skills, commercial or technical or interpersonal (for example, leadership) skills. Again, this is something you could consider even if it is not a formal condition of your research funding. These opportunities are not necessarily easily come by, so even the process of seeking them out may be both revelatory and developmental. If you have a particular career in mind, for which your current research is intended as a qualification, then you might seek voluntary work within that field to hone transferable skills, make useful contacts, add to your CV, and to aid discussions and demonstrate interest during job interviews.

Voluntary work in other sectors can also contribute to those benefits; for instance you may be able to offer your research expertise to a special interest group, or act as a guide and learning resource to children in museums and art galleries. (You must acquire a Criminal Record Bureau certificate if you intend to work with children or vulnerable adults, even though it may be on a voluntary basis.) Another option is to volunteer services of various kinds in hospitals or for charity organisations. All of these choices provide opportunities to learn and extend your skill repertoire. We will note, as the chapters unfold, which skills can benefit from such experience. These alternative activities also provide, if carefully selected, variety in your life, a chance to sometimes be someone other than a researcher.

Another set of sources of skill development opportunities are seminars, talks, workshops and conferences provided by professional bodies (such as the Royal Psychological Society, The Law Society), institutes (such as the Institute of Physics or Architects or Linguists), learned societies (such as the Geological Society, Society for Research in Higher Education, the Royal Society, the Royal Society of Arts or the Royal College of Surgeons) and associations (such as the British Educational Research Association, the American Educational Research Association, the Association of Engineers). Try to attend some of such events in your field with a view to observing carefully (listening and watching) how: presentations are delivered, questions are asked, people interact. Gather information about language use, tenor, tone and culture, then, when you feel brave enough, ask some questions, talk to others, start to become a member of the community. Find out more about developing interpersonal skills such as used in networking in Chapters 6 and 7.

Keeping motivated

It will come as no surprise that being a researcher is not continuously exciting and stimulating. It often is, but any activity carried out to the exclusion of others becomes monotonous, while there are some aspects of research that demand attention to tedious detail. For instance, while collecting data or information of any kind is often quite an adventure, preparing it for analysis can be time-consuming, lonely and boring. Interspersing such tasks with a skill development activity can keep you enlivened and give you an opportunity to meet others (and perhaps have a good moan) before going back to your desk or lab bench to pursue your research.

In contrast, when your research is going well, when you are moving forward on the crest of a wave, it can be hard to summon up the motivation to attend the course that you had booked to prepare you for the next stage in your research or in your career. If you courteously cancel, then you could take that opportunity later. However, if you are simply reluctant to attend a course/read a book/engage in other skill-developing activities because you cannot see an immediate pay-off or it is a cold day or you are feeling a bit low, it is worthwhile checking your skills inventory list or your personal development profile/record to see your current progress and encourage you to do more. Remember, also, that making a commitment to a friend or colleague to do skill development activities together may be enough to motivate you. Further, you will have a companion to share celebratory refreshment with afterwards as a reward!

You might find it useful at this point to try out Activity 3.2 to begin to create a list of possible opportunities to add to as you continue reading.

ACTIVITY 3.2   PREPARING A LEARNING ACTIVITIES RESOURCE LIST

If you have not already done so, make sure that you acquire any information leaflets from your department, faculty, and institution about training opportunities that are available. Keep this in a convenient file or pinned to your notice board to help you make the best of those resources once you have identified your learning needs.

You could also create a list of potential external learning and developmental opportunities and/or contacts that might help you to address particular learning needs. This is a good start to building your networks. You can add to your collection any advertisements you spot for voluntary or paid work to give you ideas about what might come in useful later, say, to develop your public engagement profile.

We are now about to focus, in the next chapters, on the different kinds of skills that come under the rubric of the adjective 'transferable', starting with those that emerge from your day-to-day practice as a researcher. We hope that we have convinced you in this chapter that there are many more avenues through which you can develop skills than simply through attending courses or reading a 'how to do it' manual. Skills, by their very nature, involve more 'doing' than reading or sitting in a classroom, even if they are cognitive skills.

Ideas for further reading

Boud, D. and Griffin, V. (eds) (1987) *Appreciating Adults' Learning: From the Learners' Perspective.* London: Kogan Page.

Bradbury, H., Frost, N., Kilminster, S. and Zukas, M. (2009) *Beyond Reflective Practice: New Approaches to Professional Lifelong Learning.* London: Routledge.

Kolb, D.A. (1984) *Experiential Learning: Experience as The Source of Learning and Development.* New Jersey, USA: Prentice Hall, Inc.

Tarrant, P. (2013) *Reflective Practice and Professional Development.* London: Sage.

4

WHAT ARE THE KEY INTELLECTUAL SKILLS DIRECTLY RELATED TO RESEARCH?

Chapter overview

This chapter discusses intellectual skills and issues directly related to research, considering:

- Subject knowledge and cognitive skills
- Research methods
- Academic literacy and numeracy
- Languages

and how you might develop your understanding of and ability related to them.

Introduction

As in previous chapters we want to recognise here that readers will have a range of past experience; in this chapter, one important source of such diversity is the discipline base on which you will be building your future research. Two common broad differentiations are between those researchers who are based in the sciences, technology, engineering, maths and medical fields, the STEMM subjects, and those based in the humanities, arts and social sciences subjects, which we abbreviate to HASS. This distinction breaks down, though, in instances in which research is multidisciplinary in nature or uses methods from one discipline area to explore topics in another. Examples of the both of these are often found in health studies, which may require physiological, psychological and sociological data. Engineering, biological sciences and psychology often usefully combine perspectives in relation to research on living and working environments, and so on.

For the purposes of this chapter, in which we are exploring skills specifically related to research, we will note those that we consider to be similar across most disciplines. We will also allude to those in which the research process differs by the place in which data is collected (either in a laboratory, in the field, or at a desk) since this will allow you to relate to those skills that you have already practised and some that you may need to acquire, whether staying within discipline or adventuring across disciplines. Although in the past you may have felt that your discipline was unique and different from the rest, you may be relieved to find just how similar are the research skills required at doctoral level and beyond in a range of disciplines.

This is fortuitous since we are focused here in looking at how you might further develop and hone your skills for use in a wide variety of circumstances in the future, whether you will continue as a researcher or move out into other realms of employment. One specialist area, though, that you will bring to the task is your subject knowledge from your previous degree/s. We will start the main body of this chapter with that topic, one with which you should feel most familiar.

Subject knowledge and cognitive skills

One disciplinary difference in relation to doctoral study is the entry level, some disciplines requiring a master's as well as an undergraduate degree, others an undergraduate degree with a 2:1 or above pass grade, perhaps, but not exclusively, at honours level. Indeed, for mature entry, often a professional qualification is considered equivalent to master's or bachelor level. This variation gives us a clue that it is not simply the knowledge acquired during previous study that is critical; rather, it is the cognitive skills developed during one kind of study or another. This assertion is reinforced when considering research that is interdisciplinary, relating to more than one branch of knowledge, or multidisciplinary, involving a range of disciplines or specialist professional areas. Researchers engaged in such research often need to engage in an intensive course to become familiar with the knowledge in an area outside their first discipline but do not need a full undergraduate course to do so because they already have the cognitive skills required. Hence we have combined these two topics, knowledge and cognitive skills, in this section.

As a researcher you will be expected to have core knowledge of the subjects that make up the discipline focus of your research, as well as a thorough understanding its key concepts. Further, you will be expected to make an effort to keep up with recent advances in the field by reading relevant journals, attending conferences and talks, perhaps those provided by your professional society, and, more informally, making an effort to track down and cultivate mentors and experts in the field. Certainly you should become, and keep sharply aware of, the key researchers in your specific field, what the 'hot' topics are and have a good idea of what is going on, and who is involved, in peripheral areas that might have relevance to or impinge on your area. We will return to this later when we discuss the technical skills (Chapter 6) that will help you do this and again when we address networking (Chapter 7), but first let us focus on your developing cognitive skills which are relevant to all disciplines.

One key cognitive skill relates to all forms of presentation of your research, be it a thesis, a viva voce defence, a conference paper, journal article or funding proposal. It is the ability to construct a cogent, coherent, logical and persuasive argument. One of us who regularly reviews and provides feedback on all of those presentation forms wishes she had a set of rubber stamps saying the following, so frequently does she raise the queries: 'Why?'; 'Rationale?'; 'Justification?'; 'Evidence?' The answers to such questions form the framework of a good argument. Activity 4.1 could be used as a template to help you polish your own future argument skills, while asking yourself the why question at every choice point in your research will result in a useful research habit. If you cannot identify a good answer to satisfy yourself, then it will be impossible to convince others.

ACTIVITY 4.1 PREPARING A PERSUASIVE ARGUMENT

Thinking of a piece of research that you recently completed or one in which you are currently involved, make notes in answer to the following questions. These notes will provide the framework of a well-prepared argument for any presentation of that work. If you are only part way through that research, you may find some answers in the rest of this chapter or in the recommended reading as you continue to develop your research and related skills.

Why are you focusing on that particular topic?

What evidence do you have that it is a relevant and useful one to explore?

How can the problem most usefully be formulated?

What kinds of answers (data/information) are needed to contribute some resolution of the problem?

Will those answers provide some knowledge we did not have before?

Why have you chosen that particular research approach and rejected others?

Why have you chosen particular research methods and techniques and why have you rejected others?

Do they fit comfortably with the research approach?

What is your rationale for choosing the particular analysis technique/s?

Is it suitable for the data you have (or will have) produced?

How do your interpretations of results link to the raw data?

What evidence do you have for your conclusions?

What recommendations derive from your research and how?

What would you do to improve such research in future and why?

A further two related cognitive skills underpin research: the ability to analyse and synthesise information. This involves, respectively, being able to break things down into their component parts to understand how they articulate with each other and the ability to put ideas together to make something new. You will have been practising these throughout your academic career but a dimension that might be new to you, as we noted in Chapter 2, is the need to learn the skills of *critically* analysing the ideas, work, and findings of others – and of your own. If you have come from a background in which facts have been presented as coming from unchallengeable experts, then this can be quite a steep learning curve. However, in everyday life you will be accustomed to evaluating the 'pros and cons', the advantages and disadvantages, the benefits and losses of a range of processes, opportunities and so on, so you have some experience of bringing 'criticality' to bear in your thinking. It does help to start by looking, first, for the good things in others' research and writing, and follow that by looking for what could be improved and how, finally checking for things that have been neglected, ignored or misunderstood. Within your own discipline area you will gradually develop a set of criteria to use when evaluating research.

However, there is an important aspect to this. Such evaluation in analytic thinking is not about opinion; it is about identifying and categorising characteristics based on evidence. It is not a matter of whether you like the style of research or, indeed, its outcomes, but whether it meets criteria recognised by the profession. These criteria are subsumed within the skills that we will address in the remainder of this chapter and others, but they are summarised simply in Box 4.1, with some questions you might ask yourself.

BOX 4.1 CRITERIA TO USE WHEN EVALUATING RESEARCH

When reviewing the work of others and developing/engaging in your own research, aspects to consider are:

The quality of the argument presented, with evidence, to support the description of the nature of the problem, choice of aims, objectives and research questions/hypotheses (*Is there a coherent, strong rationale for doing the research?*);

The practicality of the aims, objectives, research questions and hypotheses selection of research approach to suit the hypotheses or research questions (*Is the research doable in the time and with the resources available?*);

The strength of the link between the aims/objectives and the research questions/hypotheses (*Will solving the latter contribute significantly to meeting the former?*);

The appropriateness of the selected philosophical approach, or paradigm, for exploring or solving the problem and meeting the aims (*Is there coherence between the purpose and the chosen approach and procedures?*);

The robustness of the research design and choice of methods/techniques to collect data (*Is there a logical, coherent plan employing methods that are justified as relevant to the paradigm and capable of producing relevant data?*);

The skill used in applying methods and techniques (*Is there evidence provided that the relevant skill is available and used in the research process?*);

The quality of the raw data, the analysis process employed and the results (*Are the data and results clearly presented and is there a data trail that substantiates claims for high-calibre raw data, appropriate analysis tools and technique, and verifiable results?*);

The verifiability and justifiability of interpretations of results (*Are the interpretations clearly linked to the results and substantiated by them?*);

Coherence of whole process (*Does the research do what it sets out to do in a logical and consistent manner?*).

You will have realised by now that if others review your research using similar questions, then you will need to demonstrate the skills required for them to respond positively. These are the skills listed at the beginning of this chapter. If you have completed an undergraduate final year research project or undertaken research as part of a master's degree, then you will have already made a start on gaining some of them. However, it is important to remember that earlier training is unlikely to have been at doctoral level and is likely to have been focused on particular designs and methods suitable for a small, bounded project within the expertise of the particular academics running the course on which you were enrolled. This is not to say that such expertise was not to a high standard but to recognise that we all, as academics and researchers, have particular biases about what we consider appropriate approaches and methods. If you already have a doctorate and it was achieved in the last 10–20 years, then you may well have had some training in many of the areas we address next but it might be worth reminding yourself of what they comprise so that you can list them later in your skills portfolio (see Chapter 8).

An issue that may not yet have struck you forcibly is that such well-honed defences, alluded to in Box 4.1, result from the possibility of differences of opinion between academics about what are appropriate research questions to ask and thence what are appropriate approaches and methods to answer them. The quotation that follows is taken from one of our contributions to the Vitae RDF Planner on the topic of 'subject knowledge' (www.vitae.ac.uk):

> All our interpretations, and those of others, are based on presuppositions about 'how things are', particularly what constitutes knowledge and what are appropriate ways of finding things out. It is relatively easy to grasp the notion that new equipment or instruments that extend our senses or ability to access or manipulate objects might result in us reviewing and challenging previously accepted wisdom. It can be difficult, though, to confront the notion that different perspectives, or paradigms of thought, can produce conflicting ideas which are each defended vigorously by their similarly qualified academic proponents. It can be a shock to discover that the course studied in your first degree was founded on a paradigm and philosophical approach with which other equally respected academics disagree. One first year doctoral student gasped: 'I hadn't realised that the "Philosophy" in "doctor of philosophy" actually meant that you had to think about what the nature of knowledge is instead of just collecting and adding to it.'

Becoming aware of alternative perceptions about or interpretations of knowledge in your own field and also those disciplines closely related to it, as well as the limitations that past and current equipment and technology have imposed on understanding, will help in the isolation of particular problems or issues requiring further research.

Relativism	Realism
Subjective perceptions	Focus on tangible things
Individual holistic experiences	Logical, causal relationships
Individual constructs about the nature of reality	Factual 'truth'
Interpretation of meanings	Objective measurement
Idiographic – pertaining to specific instances	Nomothetic – generating laws

FIGURE 4.1 Comparison of relativism and realism

Paradigm choice can be an intellectual minefield because, although you may have philosophical inclinations or commitments of your own (related to your epistemology – that is, what you believe knowledge is), you also have to consider the paradigms of choice of your co-workers (supervisor, PI, advisor, research team) and what the eventual users of your research will find credible. If this debate is new to you, then you might be intrigued by the comparison in Table 4.1 between Relativist and Realist perspectives.

This you can follow up in the suggestions for further reading at the end of this chapter, bearing in mind that a relativist perspective frequently relates to what is sometimes called 'qualitative' approaches and methods, while realist approaches tend to use 'quantitative' approaches and techniques. These are short-hand labels, derived from the type of data that is usually collected within those approaches, which mask a wealth of alternatives so there is much to learn whether you are new to research or already have some years of experience. Paradigmatic identification and its links to aims, objectives, research questions and hypotheses are also addressed in Chapters 5 and 6 of another book in this Series: *Developing Research Proposals*.

The choice of paradigm in which to work should, for consistency, determine the range of research methods that you might use.

Research methods

You may be fortunate enough to have in your institutional Graduate School or Researcher Training Centre, or within your faculty or department, a programme of methods training that deals with a range of methodological issues to help you develop relevant knowledge and, perhaps, practical skills. If not, or if that learning experience was some time in the past, then you might find helpful the methods books recommended at the end of this chapter. We recognise, as we trust you do, that knowing *about* methods needs to be followed by practice in using them, accompanied by feedback to help you hone your expertise. As we mentioned in Chapter 3, you may need to seek out practical experience with the help of your supervisor/principal investigator or researcher training team. Peers can also be helpful in either sharing their skills with you or letting you use them as guinea pigs to practise some of the interpersonal methods, such as interviews or repertory grid elicitation, used in HASS disciplines.

If you are researching in a STEMM subject area, then you may have joined a group that has already identified a research problem area and is fairly confident that they know the methods required to address it. Then your prime task is to carve your own particular focus from the general one through recourse to finding a specific gap in the literature. Then ensure that you seek out guidance and support in constructing the design and using the techniques and technology required. However, beyond the doctorate, future employers, whether within or external to Higher Education, will expect that you will have acquired expertise in both selecting approaches, methods, designs and applying a range of techniques and tools. You must, therefore, in situations with a pre-organised research project, make an effort to explore the whys and wherefores of choice of topic, approach and methods so that you can construct your own methodological argument. Such an exploration should include challenging the choice in a professional way so that you can construct not just an argument for your selection, but also for your rejection of alternatives.

If you are researching in a HASS discipline, then it is more likely that you will be expected to isolate your own topic/problem for research, using your subject knowledge and library skills, and then identify a suitable approach, design and methods. As above, you must then be able to defend that selection (and exclusion).

If you are working across different disciplines, then you may need to adapt to the approaches, methods and techniques used in a different discipline to ensure throughout the research compatibility of approach and methods. You will also need to hone your argument in such a way that it satisfies a greater range of perspectives on what makes good research. Talking to others who have engaged with multi- or interdisciplinary work and reading their proposals/journal articles will help you to see the style required even if their work is quite different from yours.

Although it is a somewhat sweeping generalisation, you are more likely to find that in most STEMM subjects (apart, for example, from theoretical physics) a deductive approach is taken in which the phenomena under investigation are defined in advance and are explored systematically, perhaps experimentally, within an existing, defined framework to test current theory by exploring hypotheses about relationships between variables. Such methods often involve equipment and measuring instruments that you will need to learn how to use proficiently.

In contrast, although a deductive approach is sometimes used in HASS subjects, you could well find that an inductive approach is more suitable if your discipline fits in that group or if you are involved in some forms of medical or psychological research in which patients' or people's perspectives are required. An inductive approach is required when you are dealing with unexplained phenomena through a process of discovery in order to build theory from data. Those data are likely to be derived from a range of techniques applied flexibly, even iteratively, to respond to research questions as they arise and are refined through the research process. Often these methods involve little equipment other than recording instruments (audio and video) since the main focus of research is not objects, other than documents, but people. Documentary analysis and elicitation of people's opinions, values, beliefs, and so on, also require guided practice to develop expertise but this is expertise of a different kind from that of manipulating equipment.

Both sets of data acquisition skills require knowledge and understanding of the techniques and considerable 'practice to make perfect'; yet once acquired, both are eminently transferable.

In either case, it is important that researchers be aware of the approaches and methods used in different paradigms and why each is appropriate for seeking different kinds of knowledge. They also should be aware of and have some capability in using a range of methods within the general paradigm or paradigms in common use within their discipline, rather than only having the particular knowledge and skills required in their specific project. You would be wise to take up any opportunities, as discussed in Chapter 3, to learn and explore alternative perceptions about research and to practise a range of methods so that you are equipped to address a diversity of research problems in the future. Many jobs in the public sector, for instance, require expertise in the collection of both qualitative and quantitative data.

Of course, data/information result from all methods, including the evaluation of artefacts, so you also must become familiar with a number of analysis techniques appropriate for the kind of data/information you collect or might collect. By 'kind' we are referring to general categories such as qualitative and quantitative data and to levels of data from nominal, through ordinal and interval, to ratio data. These are terms that you will find in analysis textbooks which will also help you to formulate a rationale for your selection of particular techniques, as appropriate. However, expertise *per se* in analysis techniques requires practice, preferably guided practice by an expert. That expert may be your supervisor or PI or may be a peer or colleague or an expert from the statistics department. It is wise to solicit that help and advice before you collect your data to ensure that these data are fit for the analytic tools available and to make sure that you have had time to practise and develop your expertise before you face the prospect of a mountain of data and little time. Even for heavily qualitative data there are computer programs that can help with analysis but these require the data to be in a particular format and you will benefit from attending courses in their use so that you prepare from the start the data in the format required.

Being able to apply any analysis technique requires some numeracy skill, while writing up your research for others to learn from requires literacy skills, so we will discuss them next.

Before that, though, you might like to begin to evaluate your knowledge and abilities in relation to research methods by engaging with Activity 4.2.

ACTIVITY 4.2   WIDENING YOUR METHODOLOGICAL HORIZONS

Below we list some contrasting terms related to forms of research and their methods. Go through the list below circling those that you are familiar with, which match the research you have already engaged in. This will leave you with some terms that you need to explore further, and should lead you then to find out more about when and why researchers might want to engage in research that fits such descriptions. You might find ideas you could bring to bear in your current research, but you should at least have a broader perspective on research following this exercise.

Research that involves:

Concrete entities	or	abstract material
Identified variables	or	unknown factors
Well-researched background	or	diffuse, unexplored concepts
Reductionist	or	holistic approach
Carefully structured design	or	exploratory, iterative design
Data that are valid and reliable	or	data that are authentic, credible and dependable
Results that are generalisable	or	transferable only in particular circumstances

Academic literacy and numeracy

When we were researching the key skills that experienced researchers thought should be included in a framework for researcher development, many involved in the consultation exercise were astounded that so many contributors had included literacy and numeracy as key skills; they assumed that these should be taken for granted at this academic level. However, reaching an academic standard in these topics is not easy. The level of vocabulary, the tone and style as well as the required content of doctoral and postdoctoral academic writing are quite different from that required from undergraduates and vary also between academic tasks, such as a crafting a doctoral thesis or a journal article, or writing books for a range of audiences and developing a research proposal for funding. All of these writings should be concise, precise and accessible to the proposed audience, specialist or non-specialist. However, each has its own peculiarities about content and structure, which may differ between disciplines. The learning required to allow you to adopt each of these styles, as appropriate, is started at master's level but takes time and effort even thereafter.

Reading successful theses and peer-reviewed articles, proposals and books in your subject area or field, while being specifically alert to how they are presented, contributes to your learning but in your early years of research that reading itself, getting used to the argument or discussion format and the sometimes arcane [*sic*] vocabulary, can be onerous enough. Each of us recalls trying to read many books in our first few years as researchers that we were sure we would never understand. We would groan as we yet again had recourse to a dictionary. Looking at some of them now, after many years in the field, it is difficult to remember what was so difficult at the time – ideas that stretched our minds then are commonplace now (epistemology, phenomenology – pft! Child's play!). Nevertheless, other books/articles remain opaque and turgid to read. These latter, though, have clearly failed the 'accessibility' test and would not make our 'recommended reading' lists.

Contrary to what some of us believed in our early years, good academic writing does not set out to confuse the reader or to show off erudition (that is, cleverness – and, by the way, arcane means mysterious – understood by few); rather, it should make the complex clear in an understandable way. This may well mean using the technical language of the discipline and of research in general when writing for an academic audience. Further, it is important to use just the right words to convey your meaning as exactly as possible to avoid misinterpretation. Therefore, a good habit to get into is having a thesaurus to hand or using the one in your computer word-processing package, and consulting it when drafting and crafting.

The mention of drafting reminds us now of another common misunderstanding about academic writing: that it comes naturally to experienced writers to start with a blank page and quickly fill it with skilfully created prose. Neither of your authors knows anyone who can do this, while all the other authors we do know produce many drafts, just as we do. Often the first very rough draft is created from notes on bits of paper and/or on our laptops, from collections of papers and books with highlighting or page markers. From this we create a more legible and coherent draft. We all then have trusted others to read and review them (usually through a reciprocal arrangement), then we re-draft, re-re-draft and polish them. Even then, when these writings are sent to editors we know that they will later return them with suggestions for improvement and, so annoyingly, with punctuation and typographical errors noted that we were absolutely sure had been eliminated.

As we shall repeat in later chapters, the answer to developing this skill of writing, like others, lies in learning to be your own worst critic while persuading others to act as constructive reviewers of your work. For those of you in the very early years of research, expect and hope that your draft chapters or articles come back from your advisors well covered with suggestions and corrections; do take note of these and try not to repeat mistakes, especially those irritating punctuation errors. Many in your position try hard to submit only very polished writing whereas it might be more helpful to you, and your advisor, to produce first a draft outline for discussion and feedback on structure, followed by a draft section to get advice on style, and so on, to build up your skill gradually. Also, and perhaps counterintuitively, do not try to force yourself to write in the sequence that the final work will take – it often helps to the writing process to start by writing a section that you feel more confident about and then fit it into your planned structure towards the last draft.

Do not despair if it takes several iterations to get the piece to an acceptable standard; this is normal practice. You might also find useful some advice that we both learnt as novice writers: for everything you write set each draft aside for at least 24 hours then review it again yourself. You will find many silly mistakes that you can then readily correct, but also you will find that you can spot missing items as well as include some new ideas that have blossomed in the interim. If you are not in the habit of doing that already, we suggest you try it with your next writing task. You could then show the next draft to a peer, not necessarily in your own discipline area, to get advice on clarity of presentation of ideas and typographical errors, before showing your work to your supervisor or PI. (Of course, these suggestions preclude leaving the task until the last minute so you should take heed of the project planning and time management advice in Chapter 6.)

You will find much more detailed advice on developing your writing skill in another book in this series: *Publishing Journal Articles*. You might find it useful at this point to try out Activity 4.3.

ACTIVITY 4.3   FINDING THE RIGHT WRITING STYLE

Whatever research stage you are at, you will by now have come across some writing in your field that you have not only found useful but which has also captivated your interest. This may be in books, journal articles or theses you have read with your current research in mind. Remembering that each genre of writing serves a different purpose and so will have some major differences in presentation, gather a few of them together and analyse them using the following criteria.

What do they have in common and in what ways are they different in relation to:

Audience characteristics?

Vocabulary range?

Sentence structure and length?

Paragraph structure and length?

Signposts within the text?

General order of sections?

Headings and sub-headings, number and nature?

This might be the beginning of a guidance template for each genre that you could elaborate on as you read and write further.

You may now recognise that all researchers have to engage in academic writing in order to share their work and bring it to the attention of those for whom it is relevant. You may, however, think that academic numeracy is only for the few, particularly those researchers engaged with STEMM subjects. We would disagree.

Clearly, those of you engaged in maths or physics research, for instance, will need a much higher level of numeracy skill than us other poor mortals, but having no numeracy skill at all is not an option, even for those who deliberately choose topics for research that require qualitative data derived from interpretive approaches and methods in order to avoid statistics. (Aha! There is no hiding place!) Many students have tried to avoid the statistics courses on Research Methods programmes in the mistaken belief that they will not need the skills related to the intricacies of statistical analysis.

However, without some understanding of what different statistical tests can do, cannot do, require in the form of data and what they can demonstrate, then an argument for their rejection as a tool cannot be formulated. In addition, when reviewing the literature on topics even in very qualitatively oriented HASS fields, there will be some articles reporting research that used numerical data with some statistical analysis. Understanding those articles and evaluating their worth is precluded if you do not understand the basic rules of statistics.

Further, you may in the future find it useful to employ mixed methods to explore a research topic, collecting both qualitative and quantitative data. You should, therefore, at the very least be familiar with descriptive statistics. Again, we will suggest some helpful and accessible books at the end of the chapter but recommend also that you seek out support in your institution – most HEIs have a central resource for advising on statistics. Such experts will explain the basics and save you from making glaring errors. The language of statistics is one of the many technical languages that researchers need to be familiar with, if not necessarily fluent in.

Languages

Language skill was another area noted by experienced researchers that came as a surprise to some RDF consultants. We include in this a range of technical languages related to disciplines, methodology including analysis, information and digital technology. This latter group is growing exponentially so, although you may be very familiar with the argot and technical minutiae of your discipline, this is one language area that requires vigilance if you are to stay current.

Foreign language skills also have their place in the researcher's quiver of attributes. At an obvious level, those of us who have English as a first or second language will recognise how fortuitous for us it is that the vast majority of academic journals are now produced in that language, but some disciplines have historically been developed from strong bases in countries with other languages (chemistry in Germany, for instance), while those studying history or classics or development of any kind in countries other than their own will benefit their research by learning the appropriate language. Sometimes reading skills alone in the language will suffice, but if you are to interact with the indigenous population, and especially if you aim to collect and understand their views and opinions, then you will need to become adept at listening to and speaking their language, and indeed become familiar with their customs and etiquette. (See also Chapter 7 in relation to working in and with other cultures.) Increasingly, funding opportunities and collaborative working depend on the ability to communicate in more than one language, so acquiring an additional language might be useful in your future career.

Less obvious perhaps to those in the UK and the USA, but strongly recognised in Europe and other countries, is the growing need for researchers to be mobile. That is, to be able to share their research endeavours and outputs with researchers from other countries, not simply at conferences but also working in their labs and libraries or with them in the field or in 'virtual teams'. In Chapter 1 we mentioned the Bologna agreement and its subsequent updates. A cornerstone of that initiative is to promote excellence in European research by facilitating the mobility of researchers in order for them to work together on projects, sharing expertise and learning from each other. Being able to speak the language of a country in which you have work opportunities or networks of like-minded colleagues is a survival skill as well as a research skill.

Many institutions now provide language courses as part of some doctoral programmes or as additional opportunities, sometimes with subsidised fees, for staff, while commercial language courses abound. However, universities have a huge resource in their students and staff who come from many nations. With a little effort you could either establish a trade with an international colleague in which the barter is your English skills for their language skills, either in a formal teaching or informal conversational mode or both, or find a group of colleagues wanting to learn a language and work together to do so, sharing all the resources you can muster: print, audio, video and live discussion. This latter would help your language skills and additionally demonstrate some organisational and interpersonal skills (see Chapters 5, 6 and 7). Organisation is a key concept in managing your information, as you will find in the next chapter.

Ideas for further reading

Black, T.R. (2001) *Understanding Social Science Research* (2nd edition). London: Sage.
Reliable and practical guide.
Bryman, A. (2012) *Social Research Methods* (4th edition). Oxford: Oxford University Press.
Comprehensive, user-friendly, good for beginning postgraduates.
Crotty, M. (1998) *The Foundations of Social Research*. London: Sage.
The major philosophical stances and theoretical perspectives in a nutshell.
Denzin, N.K. and Lincoln, Y.S. (2011) *The SAGE Handbook of Qualitative Research* (4th edition).
London: Sage.
A comprehensive anthology – detailed with many further references per topic – and useful for a life-time of research.

Gray, D.E. (2009) *Doing Research in the Real World* (2nd edition). London: Sage.
Practical, comprehensive and accessible.
Greener, I. (2011) *Designing Social Research: A Guide for the Bewildered*. London: Sage.
Jargon-free guidance highlighting the key debates.
Jarvie, I.C. and Zamon-Bonilla, J. (2011) *The SAGE Handbook of the Philosophy of Social Sciences*. London: Sage.
A valuable reference source for the inexperienced and experienced alike.
Kumar, R. (2011) *Research Methodology: A Step-by-step Guide* (3rd edition). London: Sage.
Quite basic and with an over-emphasis on quantitative approaches, but accessible for real beginners.
LaFollette, H. (ed.) (2006) *Ethics in Practice* (3rd edition). Oxford: Wiley-Blackwell.
Practical and accessible.
Shafer-Landau, R. and Cuneo, T. (2007) *Foundations of Ethics* (3rd edition). Oxford: Wiley-Blackwell.
Comprehensive and authoritative.

5

WHAT SKILLS ARE INVOLVED IN DEALING WITH INFORMATION AND WITH MAINTAINING INTEGRITY AS A RESEARCHER?

Chapter overview

This chapter discusses:

- Research information and data management
- Search strategies and techniques
- Reading critically
- Copyright, attribution and plagiarism
- Co-authorship
- Ethics
- Professional integrity
- Legal requirements
- Intellectual property rights (IPR)
- Important Acts of Parliament

Information skills

Research information and data management

All research is based to some extent on acquiring, evaluating, interpreting and disseminating information and/or data, so having a clear understanding of how you interact with different kinds of information will help you to become a well-informed, information literate researcher. Being information literate is not just about evidencing good library skills, although that is a key component; you also need to understand how information and data are created and to develop a responsible (and ethical) approach to your own information management. You may find helpful a booklet referenced below (Bent et al. 2012), which informs and elaborates on the summary provided here to help you begin to devise a structure within which to plan your personal information literacy development.

As well as gathering your own primary data, your research must be undertaken within a broader information context right from the start. This not only justifies the relevance of your own work within your discipline and enables you to identify gaps in the knowledge base, but also ensures that you are as well informed as possible about your research topic.

Your search strategy and techniques

Most people can find 'some' information to inform their work, but they may not take the time to reflect on their search process and how this impacts on what they have discovered. At this level, just finding 'something' is not good enough; you need to be confident that you have found the very best, highest quality information and that you have not missed anything. For this reason, relying on a general search tool, such as Google, is clearly not sufficient. While it is true that Google can increasingly find a lot of high-quality information, it is a very random approach to a systematic literature search. You cannot tell what is missing or identify information which is not freely available and has to be paid for, or is hidden behind firewalls. A search engine can only index a very small proportion of the digital information available and the top results can be manipulated by the way in which the metadata is handled. You cannot be sure therefore that the results which come to the top have not been subtly weighted in some way. For HASS subjects in particular, not all information exists in digital form and more 'old-fashioned' library skills may need to be employed to discover it.

To ensure that you have undertaken a comprehensive literature search, it helps to develop a clear search strategy before you begin. You can do this in a structured way, by using a template such as the one we provide in Activity 5.1. Keeping notes of your search process throughout your research will help you to go back to sources systematically if a new strand develops in your research, or if you think of new keywords. You will need to revisit your search strategy regularly throughout the course of your research, being flexible and reflective to refine and adjust it depending on your results. Having control over your information behaviour in this way will also help you to justify your sources when writing up your work. Be aware, too, that new/better/different resources may appear so make sure you stay in touch with your librarians throughout your research and maintain a regular check to capture new literature as it emerges.

ACTIVITY 5.1   STRUCTURING YOUR SEARCH PROCESS

Research pro-forma

Consider the questions and topics below and record your initial ideas, thoughts and comments.

Research topic

- What is your research about?
- List keywords and phrases, alternative words, broader and narrower terms, related terms and subjects.

Research scope

- Can you identify any boundaries or limits to your research? Are there any limits by dates, location, language, methodologies, etc.?
- What type of information will help? For example, academic papers, statistics or data, images, official documents and so forth.

Current knowledge

- What do you already know?
- Where have you already looked?

Sources of information (ask your Librarian to advise on what is available to you)

- Can you list databases and electronic journals that index your subject area?

Sources of information – Specialist sources

- Do you need any other specialist sources? For example, audio resources, newspapers, scores, images, data sources, etc.

Sources of information – Primary sources

- What primary sources do you need? For example, archives, interviews.

Sources of information – Specific websites

- Are there any specific websites, as distinct from journal articles in digital form, that you need? For example, company, organisational websites.

Sources of information – People and events

- Do you need to contact people, attend events, etc.?
- Are there key authors whose work you need to read?

Keeping up to date

- How will you keep up with new information as it is produced? For example, will you use a database alerting service, mailing lists, blogs, social networking, etc.?

Anything else?

- Are there any special considerations? For example is your research based in a different country, or might you need sensitive data?

Reprinted with kind permission of Moira Bent

Once you have a clear vision of what you are looking for, applying thorough search techniques will help you to focus your search and save you time by ensuring that your information-seeking targets what you need (see Figure 5.1 below). Look for the Advanced Search options in databases and search engines and use their functionality to combine keywords in different ways (for example, you may want to search the full text of every article or to look for keywords in the title and indexes). Apply the limits you have devised (for example, date and language) and look for opportunities to focus your search by adding additional keywords.

The disadvantage of having a well-developed search strategy is that you will inevitably discover more information than you can easily cope with. Initially, you can manipulate your search results by relevance, or by date, or sorting by the most highly cited articles; this can also help you to identify key authors to add into your search strategy. Once narrowed, you can apply some general evaluative techniques to the results to ensure they are good quality sources:

- Authority – ascertain the credibility, expertise and reputation of the author(s);
- Purpose and suitability – consider who the intended audience is, and whether this might introduce a bias, and the relevance of the content;
- Date – make sure you know when the material was written in case its age and currency affect your research;
- Content – check if original research data is included, so that you can verify conclusions, and if it includes references.

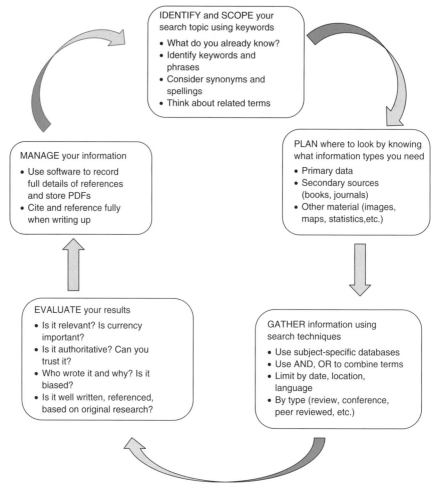

FIGURE 5.1 Search strategy diagram

Reading critically

Even after applying a logical search strategy the volume of information you have to read may be overwhelming; you need well-developed critical reading skills to enable you to sift through the information and to focus on the key material. There are three stages to the critical reading process. First, scan through the text to get a general feel of what it is saying, aiming to gain a general understanding of the information, ideas and opinions. Next, re-read to better interpret the underlying meaning of the text as a whole, identifying patterns of information, values, assumptions and language use. Finally, apply your own knowledge and values to analyse and evaluate the material and decide how you can use the information. When evaluating the material, consider the robustness of the argument and the quality of the evidence used to support it, as noted in Box 5.1.

Copyright, attribution and plagiarism

Learning to find relevant information is only part of your development as an informed researcher. You also have a responsibility to act with integrity, particularly with regard to issues such as copyright, intellectual property and attribution. As a 'consumer', ensure that you are aware of copyright law: what you may legally download and copy. Copyright applies to all printed and public materials (literary, dramatic, musical, artistic works) that have been produced by independent creative effort so will affect all researchers in one way or another. Copyright bestows on the creator/author certain rights about how the material can be used, copied, performed, broadcast, and so on. In the UK, for example, the fair dealing clause of the educational licence allows you to photocopy a maximum of 5% of a work; more than this constitutes an infringement. Copyright protection is automatic on production of the original; there is no need for registration. Therefore you need to be meticulous when quoting the work of others; even the notes provided by lecturers are copyright to them (see also intellectual property below).

Paying careful attention to citation and referencing is crucial, so developing a system to file and manage all the information you find is essential. Lazy citation, such as misattribution, incorrect referencing or, at worst, non-acknowledgement, is often caused by researchers failing to keep clear research notes of a source or concept. Save yourself time and avoid accusations of plagiarism by managing your sources efficiently, perhaps by using a bibliographical software tool to record reference details, store documents and help with accurate citation. Managing resources can be a highly complex matter and there is no shame in asking a more experienced colleague for help. Usually your library will have leaflets on this, if not special sessions devoted to such matters, but also check the conventions in your department/discipline, since these vary. It will be especially difficult to get to grips with the UK requirements if you are an international researcher and have experienced a teaching and learning environment where quoting the work of others is seen as flattering, appropriate, even with only cursory attribution, and a writing convention. Although most researchers understand that plagiarism is a serious offence, where problems do arise, it is usually because a researcher has not fully understood how to avoid it.

As a 'producer' of new information, you must also be aware of how issues of copyright and intellectual property affect you as an author. Do not assume that, just because you have written an article, for example, you will be the copyright holder and can disseminate it as you wish (see Legal requirements section below). Increasingly, researchers in the UK will be bound by the mandates of their funding bodies, which may stipulate that any outputs of funded research are published as 'open access'.

Open access material is free at the point of use, meaning that the general public and researchers in developing countries can get free access to high-quality information. Payment is made at the point of publication, passing the cost back to authors, institutions and funders. In ethical terms, making information free to all has to be seen as a positive development, but it can cause problems, especially for inexperienced authors. Before submitting material for publication, you may need to ensure that you, or your organisation, have funding in place to pay any open access charges which may be applicable. At the very least, try to sign licence agreements allowing you to deposit a version of your work in an open access repository. This is a rapidly developing area, so ask for advice from librarians and other experts.

Co-authorship

Co-authorship does not happen in all disciplines but where it does, it can be a source of difficulty among junior and senior researchers. On the one hand, it is a good way of learning how to publish in the early stages of one's career; indeed, as a doctoral researcher you may be delighted to co-author a paper with your supervisor if you feel ready to begin publishing. On the other hand, it can generate ill feeling if not handled carefully and the order of attribution, especially in large teams, can be a source of resentment if there is a perception that order of presentation of authors does not represent credit due. This is a topic on which academics may have strong feelings: the authors of this book, for instance, not only enjoy co-authoring but find stimulation in the process. They have, though, heard of instances in which senior colleagues insist on being included as authors even though they may have contributed little, if anything, to the written product, either simply because of discipline convention or as a result of the pressure for publications for research evaluation exercises. Others, like us, find such unwarranted attribution an anathema, although they recognise that there are instances when the inclusion of a prestigious name as second or third author can ease the route into publication in a high-ranking journal for those early in their research career. We would suggest that you check with your senior colleagues what expectations about joint publication prevail in your own research environment and how you can work productively and amicably within them.

Ethics

Ethics is a term usually applied to the philosophical study of moral principles. There are a number of theoretical perspectives on this issue, just as there is variation in methodological perspectives. If you are not familiar with the perspectives of teleology, utilitarianism, deontology, covenantal and critical philosophy then you may be interested to explore them later, but for now recognise that perspectives on moral and ethical behaviour are culturally and socially defined. Since the mores of any context also change with time, what was considered ethical behaviour in the past or in another context may no longer be considered acceptable now, in your context; for example, only a few decades ago 'covert observation' was considered a perfectly acceptable technique in psychology whereas now, despite the proliferation of CCTV cameras in public places, specific ethical guidelines are in place to restrict it as a research technique. However, in all contexts, and throughout history, there has been a general need within research for a code of conduct which sets out the obligation on researchers to perform their research in what is considered a professional way.

While it is important for you personally to examine what you believe is appropriate conduct, and to engage in what you consider to be principled rather than simply expedient action, you also must ensure that, at a minimum, you conform to the codes of ethics of your institution, your sponsor and any professional bodies connected to your discipline. If you are not already familiar with these codes, you should urgently make it your business to become so, checking relevant websites as a first step. This is especially so if your research involves humans or animals in any way, but even when your research is concerned with theory or only inanimate objects, including historical archives, you must consider what implications your research process and results might have for living beings.

The protection of human safety must be of paramount concern but there are other issues covered by ethics codes of practice. The idea is not simply the avoidance of harm but a striving to be morally good. In brief, a researcher should ensure that there is no dishonesty, deception, exploitation, coercion or bias involved in the conduct of the research. Instead, it should be characterised by: empathy and trust; respect for diversity and difference; and efforts to ensure that anyone involved in any way with the research understands what it is about and for, and what their role in it is. As part of your institutional code of research conduct there will be specifications and, probably, official forms to be completed, about standards for informed consent and special procedures for cases where that might be difficult to obtain, for instance when working with children or vulnerable adults. There will be specifications, too, about anonymity, confidentiality and the coding, curation and safe storage of data.

One of the things that you must do as soon as you have a good draft of a research design is to check whether it needs to be subjected to a formal ethical process, that is scrutinised and agreed by your institution's Ethics Committee, and that of your sponsor, and perhaps the regional Health Ethics Committee. These processes can be complex and time consuming, so a useful first step is to find a helpful person with prior experience to guide you through the forms and process.

Often you will also need to demonstrate in your application to an Ethics Committee, or in other ways to your sponsor, senior academic or researcher or examiner, that you have addressed related issues such as legal requirements, observance of health and safety procedures (see Chapter 6) and other professional necessities, such as abiding by copyright, attribution and Intellectual Property Rights (IPR) conventions.

REFLECTION POINT 〰

You might find it useful to think about your current or proposed research in terms of whether it might involve:

- any sensitive areas that might cause stress or embarrassment to others;
- physically demanding or dangerous, risky aspects for others;
- infringement of rights or disrespect;
- revelation of private data;
- coercion, explicit or implicit, or misleading, deceptive information about process and intentions.

If you have any suspicion at all that any of these might apply, then seek guidance about how they must be dealt with.

Professional integrity

Demonstrating professional integrity is more than simply being familiar with the theory, obeying guidelines and rules, and 'doing ethics forms'. It is about displaying awareness of the rights of all others related to research and work: colleagues as well as research participants; those upon whom research will impact as well as those engaged in its process. It is about being mindful of the environment in which research takes place as well as the people and other creatures in it.

In order to engage in appropriate practice you should be clear about the principles that guide your action, principles about honesty and reliability, and what expectations you have about your own conduct and that of others around you. There has been considerable national and international debate about appropriate practice in research in recent years; for example in the UK, the Research Councils UK (2009/11) produced *Policy and Guidelines on the Governance of Good Research Conduct*, and the Universities UK (2012), *The Concordat to Support Research Integrity*. Both documents provide researchers with guidance, but we recommend becoming familiar with the RCUK principles, no matter where you conduct research, since this document provides guidance on both what should and should not be done. It specifies the following as unacceptable conduct, and provides more detail about how these behaviours are expressed in practice: fabrication; falsification; plagiarism; misrepresentation; breach of duty of care, whether deliberately, recklessly or by gross negligence; improper dealing with allegations of misconduct.

You should make every effort to ensure that you do not make up research results, fiddle with them to make them fit a hypothesis, copy others' work, suppress data that does not agree with your ideas, fail to get informed consent, put others in danger or ignore complaints about infringements. You should be an ethical person who does research rather than a researcher who obeys rules so that, as you pursue the academic freedom of engaging in research that you can argue as relevant, you do not thereby abuse others' freedom and well-being.

However, not all issues are clear cut so that you may find yourself balancing choices in ethical dilemmas. For these, there are no easy training routes but it does help to discuss such problems with peers and seniors; in fact you would be remiss not to. Some universities hold workshops to discuss ethical principles and how to work with integrity, which may provide case studies to demonstrate how others deal with these issues.

Legal requirements

Intellectual Property Rights (IPR)

In addition to availing yourself of national codes of good research conduct, as noted above, you should also seek out the rules and requirements locally about IPR from experts in your discipline, department and institution. The rules on IPR are a minefield, particularly if you are likely to be involved in anything that exploits someone else's intellectual property as well as your own.

If you have been sponsored to do some research or you are working on a project paid for by an external body (a research council or industry, for example) you will need to establish what you are able to discuss or publish about the project and its results in the future. It could be that you find yourself unable to report anything that you have worked on, so you need to be certain of what is expected of you and which bits of the research you actually own. Similarly, you will need to be mindful of what visitors may see or have access to should they come to your office or lab.

A frequent academic error is to publish ideas and findings prematurely. Although there is an imperative to publish research findings, you could check with your enterprise section or legal advisor if you think there might be other applications of your work before you publish; for instance you might consider whether they could be patented, expanded as an enterprising idea and/or become financially viable sources of income for either you or your institution.

Important Acts of Parliament

In the UK, *ALL* researchers are subject to the Data Protection Act (DPA), which means taking very good care of the data or information you collect/ uncover during the course of your research and what you do with it afterwards. This especially applies to information that involves other people, alive or dead, and if you have information relating to individuals (their names, contact details, personal interview data, etc). It makes no difference if the information is stored electronically or on paper; as the researcher you are responsible for its safekeeping and ensuring it is disposed of appropriately at the end of the project, or retained for a specific time period if that is applicable. If you do not keep your research data/information in accordance with the DPA, this could lead to difficulties such as complaints, disciplinary action or criminal prosecution. Once a thesis has passed and is published in the UK it can become subject to questions and requests under the Freedom of Information Act (FOI). You should be aware that an embargoed thesis may not be exempt under the FOI, so you will need to be clear about what is embargoed and the reasons why, and for how long. Take advice about how this might be affected by the FOI if you intend to invoke this clause.

The way you respect your data, your informants/interviewees (if appropriate) and any confidentiality issues, and the way you record and then publish your findings reflect your conduct as a professional researcher and you will also have obligations and professional responsibilities to those who contribute data in any form to your research, your department, institution and discipline. There are lots of disciplinary and cultural variants and numerous implicit rules, so you need to ensure you are familiar with what is expected and normal practice in your area, while the Research Information Network (RIN – see Ideas for further reading) can be a useful resource in this respect. It is always best to ask for feedback and guidance if you are unsure or simply need some reassurance that you are doing the right thing.

Ideas for further reading

Bent, M., Gannon-Leary, P., Goldstein, S. and Videler, T. (2012) *The Informed Researcher*. Cambridge: Careers Research and Advisory Centre (CRAC) Limited. Available online from Vitae at: www.vitae.ac.uk/researcherbooklets (retrieved 25/09/2013).

Research Councils UK (2009; updated 2011) *Policy and Guidelines on the Governance of Good Research Conduct*. Swindon: RCUK. Available online at: www.rcuk.ac.uk/documents/reviews/grc/goodresearchconductcode.pdf (retrieved 26/4/2013).

The *Research Information Network* (RIN) supports the development of effective information strategies and practices for the UK's research community. Their website contains reports and lots of useful information for researchers: www.rin.ac.uk/ (retrieved 14/4/2013).

Universities UK (2012) *The Concordat to Support Research Integrity*. London: UUK. Available online at: www.universitiesuk.ac.uk/highereducation/Documents/2012/TheConcordat ToSupportResearchIntegrity.pdf (retrieved 26/4/2013).

6

WHAT ARE THE KEY PRACTICAL RESEARCH PROJECT SKILLS?

Chapter overview

This chapter discusses practical skill areas, including:

- Communication skills
- Networking and professional profiles
- Building reputation and esteem
- Project management
- Time management
- Health and safety

and how you might develop them.

Introduction

As a result of conducting research, there are a number of notable practical attributes a researcher should have acquired as they emerge from a doctorate, alongside increased subject knowledge and improved skill in the design and delivery of research. Although different stakeholders will place varying degrees of emphasis on which skills matter the most, they will all be transferable in one form or another to work beyond the doctorate. For instance, some might view project management and time management as most important, while the ability to communicate effectively, give a good presentation (if not a lecture) and network might be cited as essential areas by others. Everyone, however, will insist on your knowing about 'health and safety', ethical issues and to have an understanding of the legal requirements and obligations surrounding research (as discussed in Chapter 5).

We would also add to the mix the way you maintain and promote your professional profile; whether that is by active audience-focused dissemination activity, for instance publications, or by passive reputation, for example by maintaining a web presence that other people can encounter, even accidentally. Taken together, these areas comprise what we term the 'key practical research project skills'.

Communication skills

The ability to communicate your ideas and present them clearly to an audience is perhaps an area in which researchers and academic staff excel, or at least hold an advantage over other kinds of professions (except, maybe, the acting profession). There are lots of opportunities to present your work and ideas to your peers, colleagues and other audiences, including 'the public' through engagement activity. This last opportunity is extremely useful because if you practise explaining your research to a ten-year-old, you should be able to communicate with a whole range of audiences – an enviable transferable skill. If opportunities to give presentations do not force themselves upon you, you can always take the initiative to hold your own seminar sessions in your department or apply to give a paper at a conference by submitting a proposal, or get involved with public engagement activities in your institution.

However, having the opportunity to present is only the first step towards a great presentation: that is only achieved with good preparation and lots of advance practice. It may take you two weeks to put the presentation together for a conference. Although you may speed up with practice, crafting ideas for a particular audience at an important event will still take time. Remember the 'Three Ps: Prepare, Practice & Perform (PPP)'. Most of your time will be spent on the first two (even jokes and adlibs can be rehearsed to come out with perfect timing! You might be amazed at how much work goes into the seemingly natural performance of a skilled professional). Your presentation must have a focus: if you only got to tell the audience one thing, what would it be? If they only remembered one thing, what would you want it to be?

Nerves plague most of us but the audience will not know whether you managed to make every point you wanted to, while often what they see is not as you expect. It is a good idea to video yourself and/or practise in front of some critical friends who can give you honest, constructive feedback. Viewing such a video is a powerful way to convince yourself that you are probably reasonably good at giving a presentation, with only a few imperfections requiring polish. For instance, most of us talk too quickly when we are nervous and are prone to fidgety gestures, so take more breaths between sentences, slow down the speed at which you talk, control the way your hands wave or any other physical distraction, and look around the room with a bit more confidence, catching people's eyes momentarily. Most audiences will be on your side and they will wait for you (up to a point) to order your thoughts. If you have practised sufficiently and are familiar with your presentation, you should be able to gradually calm down, relax and even enjoy your experience.

As you become a more advanced presenter, you may want to develop your public speaking techniques, such as the use of rhetoric, humour, voice projection, oratory techniques and devices such as 'a hook', to obtain audience interest. There is lots of advice on public speaking available and we have listed a few useful resources at the end of this chapter.

In relation to presentation content, clearly, between the intention, the utterance (from the speaker) and the received message (by the listener) there is considerable opportunity for misunderstanding! It is always wise to check that your message has been understood and received in the way you intended it to be rather than assume perfect transmission. Indeed, 'close readings', clarifying specific points and confirming details are things researchers should practise as good communication essentials. Notice particularly the words 'clarifying' and 'confirming' above: it is important to build into your talk some repetition or redundancy because none of us can listen attentively to every word a speaker says. Thus it is easy to miss out things as well as to mishear or misinterpret them, so keep in mind the simple phrase: if it is really worth saying once, then say it twice but in another way.

REFLECTION POINT 〰

Observe television news broadcasts and note how they begin with the 'headlines', followed by 'the story' and then close the broadcasts with 'the summary'. Can you organise your next presentation in a similar way?

Networking and professional profiles

There is an old saying, 'out of sight, out of mind', which was updated by Dr Bruce Heller to 'Outta sight, outta mind ... outta business!' (Frankel 2004: 123). This applies as much to academia as it does in the business world. If people are not aware of your work or research contributions, why should they shortlist you for that academic post against the other 50 candidates who applied?

It is essential for an academic career as much as it is in other kinds of work that you communicate your work and raise your professional profile through:

- planning a dissemination strategy;
- networking with other professionals in the field;
- promoting your professional profile via a range of media.

Your dissemination strategy (a plan of what to disseminate and when) should be established at the beginning of every research project and reviewed regularly with your supervisor/PI or mentor, checking for disciplinary conventions. Some disciplines, law for example, may not require PGRs to be published by the time they finish their doctorate; others, particularly in engineering and the sciences, will find that they publish as part of a group effort as a matter of course; among HASS researchers, it may be down to the individual PGR with supervisory advice to ensure they are published, especially if that is a requirement for the next academic post. However, all ECRs will need to devise a dissemination strategy for their work.

Whatever your field, it is important to discuss with your supervisor/PI exactly what you intend to publish in case it compromises your claim to an original contribution to knowledge (for doctoral students) or any intellectual property agreements if you are member of research staff.

Networking and social networking are essential tools for researchers. They are the means for generating and exchanging ideas, finding collaborative partners and are good vehicles for promoting your professional profile, reputation and esteem. Academic sites are increasing, while LinkedIn, for example, has become the equivalent of 'Facebook' for business and professional people, so, if you are looking for a job, having a profile on LinkedIn may help bring you to the attention of a wider range of people than exist locally. The growth and use of online and virtual working will change Higher Education considerably in the near future. Whether your use Twitter, Facebook, LinkedIn or other online media, it is critical you control your image and build a professional profile. Prospective employers (including academic ones) may check out your Facebook page or 'google' you to see what comes up. We do not want to stifle your creative comments, but we suggest you monitor your privacy levels and ensure that everything is appropriate for the (potential) audience who may access it.

You need to take care of your public and professional image. It is a good idea to regularly review what is being held publically about you through searching for your name on the internet and checking whether you would be comfortable with the most eminent professor in your field reading it prior to an interview! However, you cannot control everything on the internet; so if there is something you do not like, at best you can ask for site owners to change it but, if they do not, you may have to simply live it down.

Networking is intended to be a mutually valuable activity – be generous rather than selfish. The internet opens up the possibility of helping others and being a global citizen (see Chapter 11). Whether face-to-face or virtual, altruism should be at the heart of your networking relationships, and this should generate reciprocity in those with whom you establish and build up a relationship; this is the route to successful and sustainable networking. If you help someone with a reference, suggest literature, a website or source of funding, share ideas and are generally useful, the chances are they will offer you useful information in return. You will need to build and cultivate your network, and keep your contacts and relationships 'warm' by up-dating information and maintaining regular contact. Your contact with others needs to be purposeful: enquiring after someone's well-being or emailing that it was nice to meet them at a conference is only the beginning of any correspondence; you need to follow it with a reason for getting in touch and maintaining the link.

Professional networkers will keep all information relating to their contacts on a database. If you receive someone's business card at a conference, it is a good idea to note some basic details on the back of the card immediately and before storing it. You never know when you might need that contact, or know someone else who does, for a reference, referee, or information about a job.

It is a good idea to develop a range of contacts in and outside your subject area and institution. Remember that external contacts, say with a large business, a public organisation, a small business and charity for example, may prove a rich source of collaborative partnerships, if not future funding. Ultimately, as Elizabeth Wilkinson of the University of Manchester's careers service pointed out, networking is not about 'who you know' but rather 'who knows you'. Try the next Activity to explore this.

ACTIVITY 6.1   WHO KNOWS YOU?

List the people who know you in the following areas:

- Your university but outside of your academic department
- UK and EU HEIs
- International educational institutions outside Europe

- The business or commercial sectors
- The voluntary, charity or public service sectors
- Government bodies or policy making
- The media
- Social media: are you LinkedIn, on Facebook, Twitter, etc.?

If you do not have any connections in some of the above categories, you need to ask yourself if that matters and, if you think it does, whether you can cultivate relationships in these areas.

From the *ECR Toolkit* (2013), cited with kind permission of the University of Southampton.

Building reputation and esteem

Clearly, your network-building efforts will contribute to your research reputation. To make certain that it also begins the long journey to establishing professional esteem, you need to ensure that your reputation for producing well-honed and interesting research is accompanied by regard for your reliability as a colleague, your integrity in research practice, your willingness to be interested in the work of others as well as your own, and for how well you balance authority with humility. Authority comes from the confidence you have in the evidence you bring to bear in a well-crafted argument, while humility derives from being willing to hold your research up to scrutiny, carefully considering alternative perspectives and critiques without becoming defensive.

These are high standards to live up to and hence not everyone who has a good research reputation is also held in esteem. However, remember that respect breeds respect so a good start would be to actively seek out and establish connections with researchers you respect, giving constructive, well thought-out feedback on their work and asking for reciprocation. Further, following up our suggestions for networking and then putting yourself forward to serve (note the word) on local, then national, or international committees related to your discipline and research area will build and enhance your reputation and contribute to your gaining esteem.

Project management

By the end of the doctorate, researchers should have an idea of the basic principles of project management, while ECRs should begin to develop a clearer sense of their own project management style. There are lots of different approaches to and models of project management (see a select few in our recommended resources at the end of this chapter), which is great news because it means everyone can find a method that suits them best.

Generally speaking, project management is concerned with maintaining control of a project to ensure a smooth flow of activity from start to finish, ideally with the minimum of stress and fuss. Essentially there are five main elements to project management (models variously contain greater or fewer elements) and these include: scoping the project; designing it; doing it or conducting the project; monitoring progress; and completing and finishing the project properly. Scoping a project establishes what needs to be done and for whom (the client), and what the project will include, such as the aims, objectives and deliverables, while it is also useful to decide what it will not cover. Once the details have been scoped out and you have determined the shape of the project, the priorities and tasks can be put in order or in the sequence in which they need to occur, and a plan drawn up which should include any dissemination strategy and budget for costs.

It may be helpful to define the end result and design the project around it, including resources, key deliverables and milestones, and place this into a realistic timeframe. Activity 6.2 below will give you some idea about scoping, identifying deliverables, designing a plan and scheduling tasks. The use of SMART (see Box 6.1) objectives is a common tool for ensuring the goals and/or deliverables are robust and likely to happen.

From the outset the stakeholders, others who might have an interest in the project and need or like to be kept informed of its progress, should be identified and sorted according to level of priority. Ascertain who needs to know what and when. Finally, every project needs a proper ending and this stage is not just for delivering the end result or outputs (for example, a thesis, paper, research findings, etc.), but also for reflecting on the process overall. This provides the opportunity to review what worked well, what could be done differently and what was learned, aside from simply fulfilling the remit. Closing the project and celebrating success can be easily overlooked but is critical for moving on emotionally and developing your transferable skills – not to mention providing useful examples for employment interviews.

ACTIVITY 6.2   AN EXAMPLE OF INFORMAL PROJECT PLANNING

Imagine that you would like to organise a surprise dinner party for a colleague and friend who has just completed their research, but you only have a budget of £50 and you know that you will need to invite at least 10 people. You want to make the event special. Can you draw up a project plan from now until the departure of the guests? For example, what would be on the menu? Are there any special considerations (food allergies, religious requirements)? Where and when will you hold the event? How will you allocate the budget? What shopping will you need to do and when? Who will do the catering? If you are going to be the chef, in what sequence will the food need to be prepared, cooked and served? Will there be additional entertainment?

Can you map the skills from this activity onto a more work-based project to demonstrate their transferability?

It is very rare for a project to run as smoothly as planned and the longer the duration of the project, the more vital the monitoring stage becomes. All kinds of things can throw a project (including research projects) off track; for example, poor design, inadequate planning of resources (time is a vital resource that is well known for rapidly disappearing), stakeholders' disagreement or undue influence, illness, or simply a lack of motivation, boredom or procrastination, can all impede progress. Unforeseen events or the inappropriate scheduling of tasks will inevitably slow progress, so the project manager needs to think and respond quickly and sometimes imaginatively. Although it would be wise to consider possible risks to the project at any one stage (and there is considerable literature on risk management alone), close monitoring will facilitate timely interventions and the correction of problems, and should avert most potential disasters.

BOX 6.1   USEFUL PROJECT MANAGEMENT TOOLS THAT CAN BE FOUND ON THE INTERNET

The '5 Whys'. This 'tool', by Sakichi Toyoda, comes from the Toyota Production System. It is an iterative approach that asks 'why?' of a problem, maps the answers and subjects these to further rounds of the question 'why?'. Useful for scoping all kinds of problems and questions, including research questions, it is especially helpful if the project becomes stuck and you are not sure what to do or where to go next.

The '5 Hows'. This tool closely follows on from the '5 Whys' above. It uses the same iterative technique, and is useful for finding solutions and designing the project.

The CIA Problem Solving Checklist or the Phoenix list. This is a checklist of questions for problem-solving and planning. Not all questions will apply to a single project, so pick out the most appropriate.

Critical path analysis. This is good for sequencing and planning a project, and is similar to the Gantt chart (see below). PERT (Program Evaluation and Review Technique) is a variation of the critical path approach.

(Continued)

(Continued)

The Gantt chart. This is useful for scheduling tasks and illustrating the phases of a project. It is very easy to make your own 'Gantt' chart for timetabling tasks.

Mindmapping is a specific technique attributed to Tony Buzan. It is used for all kinds of activities, including creating shopping lists and planning holidays!

Root cause analysis. This may help you to understand the underlying and deeper causes of problems.

SMART is the acronym 'Specific, Measurable, Attainable, Relevant and Time-bound'. It is a simple and useful interrogative tool to make objectives robust and less vague.

SWOT analysis looks for the 'Strengths, Weaknesses, Opportunities and Threats' of a project or situation. SWOT can be useful for monitoring projects as well and testing their robustness.

To-do lists. These are a simple way to prioritise tasks.

Commercial software. Microsoft Project is useful for managing projects and scheduling tasks of all sizes. Prince2 is an expensive software package for large and complex projects; it is the tool of choice for CEOs of organisations.

Time management

Simply put, time management is about working 'smarter not harder' – so that you have more time for the fun things! As with project management above, time management concerns being highly aware of your behaviour; that is, how you use your time and how to exercise greater control over it. Most of us are only vaguely aware of how we spend our time. For instance, do you really know how much time you spend emailing or surfing the net on non-research related pursuits per week? Activity 6.3 will enable you to obtain a more realistic view of how you use your time and help you think about reducing any 'time wasters'.

ACTIVITY 6.3   TIME MANAGEMENT WEEKLY LOG

Make a template similar to the one below and log your use of time for at least three days or, ideally, a whole week. Record your main activities at regular intervals during the day, such as every hour or half hour; include eating, watching television, emailing, etc. Once you have completed your log, address the additional questions and activities.

Sample time log:

Time	Day 1/ Monday	Day 2/ Tuesday	Day 3/ Wednesday etc. ...
7.00–8.00	Record of activity ... *Breakfasted, showered, dressed.*	Record of activity ...	Record of activity ...
8.00–9.00	*Drove to work*		
9.00–10.00	*Team meeting*		
10.00–11.00	*Email – correspondence (45 minutes) Tea break*		
11.00–12.00 Continue adding time slots for the day	*Started to read report* *Dealt with interruptions (20 minutes) ... and so on ...*		

Once you have recorded your activities, you can review your time log for your key activities and the total number of hours you spent on them. For example, the total time you spent:

In meetings =

Emailing =

Reading =

In the lab =

Doing domestic chores =

Watching the television =

Other =

Now answer the following questions:

- Are there any obvious surprises in the way you use your time?
- Are you satisfied with how you use your time?
- What are your main time wasters?
- Is the balance right between work, home and leisure?
- What do you want to spend less time on?
- What would you like to devote more time to?

Can you reorganise any activities? Can you distinguish between important and urgent tasks to prioritise your activities?

Time logs are useful in identifying any time-wasting or time-consuming (things imposed on you) patterns and where you could organise yourself more efficiently. Managing your time better requires being honest (or ruthless) over prioritising what needs to be done and/or seeking more efficient ways of doing tasks. If time is short it is best to focus on the things that make a difference or really matter; there may be little point spending time on tasks that reap no reward, or you enjoy doing but are not very productive; alternatively, it may be possible to make better use of unproductive time, such as travelling for example. Another good tip is simply to say NO to distractions. Saying no becomes easier with practice.

It is useful to review your use of time regularly to see if any other kinds of time wasters have crept into your way of working. One of us spends 2 hours a day travelling to and from work; this becomes 10 hours a week spent in a car, or 40 hours a month. Imagine what could be done with an extra 40 hours or one whole working week! She could improve her language skills listening to a CD in the car, or gain valuable time for reading an article or writing a paper if she could travel by train. If she worked from home one day a week this would amount to a saving of 96 hours in a year (based on saving 2 hours per week × 4 weeks × 12 months) or around two whole weeks of extra research time. Think what could be achieved with that!

Time management tools or tips include:

- Using 'to do' lists and prioritising tasks according to their level of urgency and importance.
- Setting aside time or blocking out time for tasks. Working in regular blocks is good for part-time researchers.
- Being strict with yourself. If you set deadlines, meet them; if you are only going to allocate a certain amount of time to a task, stick to it (if you have not completed the task you may need to review your project management skills – see above).
- Doing boring tasks when you are tired and thinking tasks when you have high energy, usually in the morning (see Activity 6.4).

ACTIVITY 6.4   *MAKING BETTER USE OF YOUR ENERGY CYCLE*

We all have high and low energy cycles during the day. On average, you should have two peaks of energy during the day. Plot your energy cycle on a table similar to the one below for two or three days to confirm consistency. Can you structure your work to use peak energy times to do critical thinking or high concentration work and do mindless or less taxing tasks, such as dealing with emails or updating your reference library, at low energy times?

Energy Level	Time of day 7am – 9am – 11am – 1pm – 3pm – 5pm – 7pm – 9pm – 11pm – 1am – 3am – 5am
High	
Medium	
Low	

Finally, the arch enemy of all work, as most researchers know, is procrastination. We are all prone to it, especially if it involves a disliked task. A useful piece of advice comes from Mark Forster (2000) (see Ideas for further reading below), who suggests facing the task and working on it for only five minutes. Think of this as a warm-up exercise; as Forster says, we can all do something for five minutes.

Health and safety

One of the authors once asked a group of new doctoral researchers in HASS what they thought the most dangerous thing was that could happen to them while working on their research projects. One witty audience member shouted out, 'A paper cut!' As amusing as that comment was, it displays a belief that health and safety matters (like ethics) only apply to certain disciplines, such as those involving, for example, dangerous substances or machinery, unsafe locations, people or animals, and only then if they are alive and not dead. So if your research involves nothing more exotic than reading books, listening to sound, or looking at inanimate objects/artefacts, then you might be forgiven for thinking that health and safety issues do not affect you. We disagree!

Health and safety procedures vary with each discipline and each department, and with the type of building or location you work in, including the evacuation procedures in the event of a potential fire, for instance. They will also apply to less obvious areas, such as the way you store your books or papers, and to working late hours. We cannot emphasise enough that it is in your best interest to find out what the rules and guidelines are for health and safety in your discipline, department, and in your office.

In addition, you need to consider your personal safety and be especially careful if you are going off-site to conduct research, to interview people for example. The authors both have examples of troublesome health and safety situations involving researchers interviewing strangers off-campus in a private venue with no one else briefed about the location and timing and in ready contact. Similarly, care and common-sense precautions are required when working late and needing to get home in the dark, or observing the behaviour of groups in a public place. In such situations you must make provision for your personal security, including being prepared for potential challenge to observation activity. (See your department/institution for guidance and The Suzy Lamplugh Trust weblink below.)

Individuals are also responsible for the health and safety of others within their own working environment, for instance by ensuring there are no trip-hazards. Such precautions would apply equally to a seminar group you might be leading as to the students in a lab and pregnant colleagues you work alongside. Health and safety responsibilities fall on us all, not just the head of department, in our working environment. You should attend to any health and safety talk or online courses provided, and be sensibly alert to what could go wrong while you are working on your research, irrespective of the location and who you are with.

Ideas for further reading

Personal effectiveness

Allan, D., Kingdon, M., Murran, K. and Rudkin, D. of ?What If! Ltd. (2002) *Sticky Wisdom: How to Start a Creative Revolution at Work*. Oxford: Capstone Publishing (A Wiley Company).

Browning, G. (2001) *Innervation: Redesign Yourself for a Smarter Future*. Harlow: Pearson Education.

Frankel, L.P. (2004) *Nice Girls Don't Get the Corner Office: 101 Unconscious Mistakes Women Make that Sabotage Their Careers*. New York: Business Plus.

Kingdon, M. of ?What If! Ltd. (2012) *The Science of Serendipity: How to Unlock the Promise of Innovation*. Chichester: John Wiley & Sons.

Presentation skills

Etherington, B. (2006) *Presentation Skills for Quivering Wrecks*. London: Marshall Cavendish.

Gallo, C. (2012) *The Presentation Secrets of Steve Jobs: How to be Insanely Great in Front of Any Audience*. New York: McGraw-Hill.

The BBC has a range of video clips on *The Speaker* at: www.bbc.co.uk/speaker/improve/ (retrieved 23/3/2013).

Toastmasters International – 10 Tips for Public Speaking at: www.toastmasters.org/tips.asp (retrieved 23/3/2013).

Project management

Barker, S. and Cole, R. (2012) *Brilliant Project Management: What the Best Project Managers Know, Do and Say* (3rd edition). Harlow: Pearson Education.
Useful for ECRs and those with some project management experience.
Posner, K. and Applegarth, M. (2008) *Project Management Pocketbook* (2nd edition). Arlesford, UK: Management Pocketbooks Ltd.
A good introduction to project management.

Time management

Clayton, M. (2011) *Brilliant Time Management: What the Most Productive People Know, Do and Say*. Harlow: Pearson Education.
Forster, M. (2000) *Get Everything Done and Still Have Time to Play*. London: Hodder & Stoughton.

Networking

Warne, J. (2000/2008) *Networking Pocketbook*. Arlesford, UK: Management Pocketbooks Ltd.

Health and safety

The Suzy Lamplugh Trust has advice on Personal Safety and Lone Working: www.suzylamplugh.org/ (retrieved 14/4/2013).
The Health and Safety Executive website has a section on education that includes Higher Education: www.hse.gov.uk/services/education/index.htm (retrieved 18/4/2013).

7

WHAT ARE THE KEY PEOPLE SKILLS AND PERSONAL ATTRIBUTES?

Chapter overview

This chapter discusses the interpersonal skill areas of:

- Attention to diversity issues
- Environmental awareness and sustainable working
- Leadership
- Managing people and resources
- Being personally effective
- Ensuring social and political survival
- Team working
- Working collaboratively

and how you might develop them.

Introduction

In Chapters 4, 5 and 6 we explored the intellectual, legal, information and practical skill areas and attributes derived directly from research, and which we believe a researcher should, by virtue of engaging in research, encounter and be able to acquire, if not improve on, during their time within an Higher Education Institution (HEI). There are two additional skill sets researchers must develop that are perhaps not readily obvious and will require a proactive approach by researchers to acquire. The first, discussed here, relates to what are often called the 'softer' key transferable skills, the skill set and attributes associated with people, interpersonal relationships and personal development. The second relates to using skills to best advantage, making the most of those you have and extending them purposefully to expand your CV, which is discussed in Chapter 11.

The notion of 'soft skills' is a difficult one to define, but this does not mean they are weak attributes, or any less demanding or less academically challenging than the other transferable skills. Although 'soft skills' are a tendentious set of attributes, generally speaking, the source of career failure or anxiety is 'rarely a shortfall in technical or professional expertise'; rather, 'it invariably stems from a shortcoming in the … soft skills repertoire – the non-technical traits and behaviors needed for successful career navigation' (Klaus 2007: 1) As Stephen Johnson and Helen McGregor (2005) indicate, 'Soft skills are hard!' You will find these publications, and others referred to in the text that follows, in our Ideas for further reading at the end of this chapter.

Attention to diversity issues

People are different in all kinds of ways and attention to diversity is about respecting others, irrespective of their visible and non-visible differences, and recognising and valuing people as individuals. A university is an extremely diverse environment that affords wonderful opportunities to develop knowledge and relationships that will benefit you in your current research and in the future. Being able to deal positively with diversity is one of the key skills required of researchers in the internationalised education environment and of global managers in all environments. Indeed, it is believed that heterogeneous groups make better decisions, so learning how to include people, knowing how to get the best from them and enabling them to contribute their unique voice are a key skill that looks set to grow in desirability by a range of employers, especially as work becomes an increasingly global and multicultural affair.

> In England, Scotland and Wales, the Equality Act (2010) protects individuals from unlawful discrimination on the basis of nine 'protected characteristics': age, disability, gender reassignment, marriage and civil partnerships, pregnancy and maternity, race, religion and belief, sex, sexual orientation. (The Equality Challenge Unit – see the website below)

Researchers everywhere need to be alert to these nine 'protected characteristics' and raise their awareness of the hidden or unconscious biases they may hold. We all have unconscious subtle preferences or prejudices which unwittingly affect the way we treat people and the decisions we make. These have repercussions in a wide range of ways, for example from the likelihood of career success, say, for women in STEMM or black and ethnic minority staff in all disciplines, to the way new colleagues are made to feel welcome by you and included in the department. Activity 7.1 below may help you think about implicit assumptions you might hold about academic behaviour. However, explicit training about unconscious bias and diversity is the best way of challenging those latent and deeply held assumptions.

ACTIVITY 7.1   WHAT DOES THE CONTEMPORARY ACADEMIC LOOK LIKE?

On a blank piece of paper or flip-chart, quickly sketch a picture of the contemporary successful academic, indicating appearance and common activities.

When your sketch is complete, look at your picture closely and see what it reveals about *your* assumptions. Have you drawn any clichés or stereotypes? You could invite a critical friend to review your picture for you. The dilemma is that we do need to have some general expectations about the world in order to deal with its complexity, but these can easily lead to discrimination, conscious or not.

One of the disappointments international researchers sometimes mention is that they wanted to share their native experiences, culture and knowledge as well as share in those of the country they are visiting, but did not have the opportunity to do so; worse, they might feel their colleagues were not interested in these things. We could all make greater effort to appreciate our colleagues, especially those from other countries, and find out more about the 'gifts' they bring. Research has always had an international dimension but it has become an intensive global activity in terms of reach and the range of researchers involved. For instance, many HEIs have institutions off-shore and virtual teams are increasingly common. In this environment, learning how to work successfully in different cultural settings and with multicultural teams is paramount. Indeed, in all probability you already work in a multicultural team or department.

There is an old proverb that courtesy opens any door but, in this era, when researcher mobility is strongly encouraged, being courteous entails finding out what is considered appropriate and good manners in other cultures as well as observing those rules of behaviour that you were brought up with. We are using 'culture' very generally here to include discipline as well as national or other large group variants. Learning from colleagues with different backgrounds through discussing cultures, customs, etiquette and pedagogic differences will provide insights useful for current and future collaborative work.

REFLECTION POINT

How can you promote diversity in your department or workplace? For example, the University of Reading doctoral community held a regular 'Culture Club' where researchers took the opportunity to explain their home countries' norms and expected behaviours. The University of Southampton offers a weekly Global Café, enabling UK and international researchers to meet informally, share experiences and network.

Environmental awareness and sustainable working

As with attention to diversity issues above, being environmentally aware and working in sustainable ways requires consideration of the broader impact of one's behaviour, ways of working and outputs. Sustainable and responsible working is similarly expected of organisations; sometimes this is referred to as 'corporate social responsibility' (CSR). CSR is not only about the usual health and safety issues, but is also concerned with behaving ethically and responsibly. Although CSR does not impact on universities with the same intensity as it does the corporate sector, the key tenets around responsible and ethical conduct have filtered through to HEIs, so we see greater use than previously of recycling, fair-trade products, and environmental impact analyses.

All businesses need to be increasingly mindful of how their processes and products impact on people and society in a range of ways, for example, by ensuring they are not polluting the environment, do not have child labour in their productions lines (or 'value chains'), and that they minimise the stress levels of their staff. The notion of sustainability extends this to how people work, how materials are sourced and produced, and takes into consideration the impact our individual and organisational work has on the environment and human well-being beyond the local to the global.

Everyone needs to be more aware of their practices and to work in a sustainable way, from the humblest researcher through to the whole organisation. It is important to cultivate such good habits early in your career as a good basis for working elsewhere.

Regularly reviewing your own research practices, such as recycling, energy use, and so on, is a good place to begin.

Leadership

It is said that leaders are made not born, which is good news because it suggests we all have the potential to turn ourselves into leaders. There is much advice for you to draw on to help you achieve this but the real test of leadership resides in the 'doing'. The assumption that you can be a leader only if you are (a) the head of an organisation or (b) in a position of authority, having been given or acquired a 'leadership' role, is misguided and outdated in our complex times. Hoping to learn leadership 'on the job' might be leaving it rather too late. Ideally, you should have developed the skills needed for the role well in advance. You do not have to wait for greatness to be thrust upon you; rather, you can generate the qualities required beforehand. You can show or demonstrate leadership at any level. Indeed, most people do not aspire to the top job early in their careers but find themselves propelled upwards precisely because of the leadership skills they have developed and demonstrated.

How can you demonstrate leadership? There is a famous distinction made by the writer and sociologist Peter Drucker (1973) that management is about doing things right, while leadership is about doing the right things. For day-to-day activity, management keeps things working but when something needs to be done, such as in times of crisis or change, leadership qualities rather than management ones are required. Leadership consists of the skills, qualities and character you exert under certain conditions, such as the ability to command loyalty and respect from others as you motivate them to engage with specific activities.

Conventional wisdom holds that you become a leader as soon as you have 'followers', which opens up the notion of leadership further. As a researcher you can lead with ideas, or 'by example' in the way you behave towards others, and you can lead in the way you step up and face challenges large or small, in how you 'do the right thing' when the opportunity presents itself. Self-reflection and working out your style will be essential in developing leadership skills; books and courses are helpful at given points, and certainly reflection or After Action Review (see Chapter 8) after an event will be useful. You need to seek out ways in which you can demonstrate and develop your leadership abilities; volunteering to lead a discussion on your research for colleagues, for example, would be a useful start.

When considering your own research leadership potential, think about other leadership roles you have had and currently already have. These are likely to be more numerous than you think. For instance, did you lead a team in a youth organisation when younger, or have you been in charge of some university social or academic groups, or a captain of a sports team?

Do you currently run a social club or work group or hobby/craft society, or have you organised a petition or set up a Parents' Forum? These and other similar activities demonstrate leadership experience that can enhance your CV and research. They will also give some indication of your leadership style(s) that might provide a foundation for the further development of your leadership potential. Whatever you do to develop your leadership style and experience, humility and self-awareness will be critical attributes.

There are numerous leadership models available. We suggest you investigate some of the following using the internet or your library:

- Action-centred leadership by John Adair consists of three elements: 'achieving the Task, developing the Team, and developing Individuals'.
- Resonant leadership: emotionally in-tune leaders create work relationships where everyone works at their best and are committed to what they are doing.
- Self-leadership: helpful for researchers who may need to develop their own contexts and style.
- Servant leadership: leaders empower and nurture their teams, and work to support them.
- Situational leadership: Paul Hersey and Ken Blanchard suggest that different situations require different leadership styles (obvious really but have you got a sufficient range?).

Influence sits alongside leadership and is another area you may need to cultivate. You can be influential without having a formal leadership role but you are unlikely to be offered such a role unless you are perceived to have some potential influence in the community. The quality of being influential is not something that you might easily recognise in yourself, nor can others bestow it on you. They can help you to be influential by giving you a title which others might recognise as indicating high status or access to power, but it is up to you to demonstrate to those you wish to influence that you have something to say that has relevance or have done or can do something that will impact upon them (preferably positively).

In relation to research, being influential means being recognised as an authority either on a research approach or method or topic, or it could mean that you are recognised as having an impact on policy or practice in relation to research. You will have to be proactive in speaking and writing about your research to reach and influence people. You need to accept, and even cajole, invitations to meetings and committees in which policy and procedures are discussed and make effective contributions to them. You may be shy but you cannot let this stop you if you want to be influential. You have to put undue modesty to one side because, sad but true, no one will simply notice how wonderful you are and insist that you take on an influential role. Activity 7.2 may help with this if you are naturally shy or, in contrast, if you sense you might be considered overweening.

ACTIVITY 7.2   DEMONSTRATING YOUR INFLUENCE

Make a list of your most important research and work achievements. You could include conference papers presented, invitations to speak at conferences, journal articles written and contributions requested, and so on.

Then use this to write a reference for yourself using the third person, as if writing about a good colleague for whom you have respect. This may help you gain some perspective, especially if you include in it some evidence to support the assertions you make.

If you then show that reference to a mentor or close colleague and ask them to review it in terms of how well it describes you, you might get a more realistic picture of the ways you might be influential already, and how you might improve on that aspect of your profile.

Managing people and resources

Although there may be few opportunities for managing people or resources as a PGR or ECR, you will be expected to manage one or both as you progress in your career within or outside academia. Therefore it would be useful to obtain what knowledge, insight or experience you can, no matter how limited that may be.

It may be difficult to acquire direct experience of managing a team or a multi-million pound budget, yet if you can gain some experience of managing people and have the opportunity to review your people skills or, better still, have someone review them for you, then this will be an excellent addition to your skill set. You could, for example, volunteer to help undergraduates or postgraduates with projects, or organise a conference with them or your peers. Budgeting opportunities may be harder to achieve, but we can all reflect on how we manage our own finances and/ or small grants, and certainly we can think about how we manage other resources in our research. You can be more effective and influential if you can make the business case for any idea or suggestion you have, so this is a useful management technique to acquire, especially if you want to persuade people. Indeed, every funding proposal and application demands skill in this area (see our series book: *Developing Research Proposals*).

Undoubtedly, learning to interact with people is one of the most rewarding and, sometimes, challenging aspects of work of any kind. It is not just about being 'in charge', but being aware of how you manage relationships in general that will be beneficial to your research work as well. Key areas to consider include: managing upwards or managing your supervisor/PI; managing sideways, that is how you conduct your peer relationships; and managing direct reports, junior colleagues and students. The most challenging area of all concerns managing conflict, difficult people and/or difficult conversations. None of the aforementioned is easy but with experience, practice and reflection we all learn to improve our skill in these areas. In addition, you can learn a lot from: mentors and role models; asking questions of more experienced colleagues; observing others; and reading key publications. Acquiring coaching skills and techniques is especially beneficial for managing or dealing with people in every kind of relationship (see Chapter 10).

Being personally effective

Being personally effective draws upon your personal qualities, such as enthusiasm or passion and perseverance (discussed below), your organisational skills and approach, and how you operate, that is how you bring all of these things together to achieve an objective or fulfil a task. At a minimum, being personally effective will help you deal with a changing and complex world, but at most it will ensure you perform well in any environment. The focus is on your working style and how you achieve goals in efficient ways. This is not simply about getting what you want, but doing so because you have made excellent use of your resources and skills. The kinds of things that determine how effective you are include:

- how you respond to work and challenges in particular;
- how you manage stress;
- your awareness of your skills and capabilities to play to your strengths;
- your consciousness of your weaknesses and your impact on others;
- how you maximise all of this to produce excellent results time after time and make a positive impact on your organisation and colleagues.

These link to influencing skills, as discussed above.

It is encouraging to know that you can learn how to behave differently and teach yourself to become more effective, while the key to improving your own performance is a high level of self-awareness.

Perseverance and passion

Two of the most frequently cited descriptors of good researchers, by the experienced researchers interviewed to produce the Researcher Development

Framework (RDF), were that they demonstrate perseverance and passion/ enthusiasm. In effect, you need to have some commitment and passion in order to persevere with research. This is because, though research may be exciting and stimulating at times, some of the time it is hard graft punctuated by problems and disappointments. Thomas Edison, famous for his light bulbs, made two observations relevant to this:

'I have not failed. I've just found 10,000 ways that won't work.'

'Genius is one percent inspiration and ninety-nine percent perspiration.'

We, along with a multitude of others, will be advising you to disseminate your research and you will find, if you have not already, that there is huge competition for journal article and conference presentation opportunities. Success, however, comes from perseverance. Where the reality is that many researchers spend much of their time, like Edison, following unfruitful, and thereby unpublishable, explorations with only occasional breakthroughs, what keeps them going is the challenge and the need to find out 'why' and 'how', the passion for painstaking detective work and the determination not to be beaten by a puzzle.

If that describes you, and it probably does since you have probably overcome many barriers to become a researcher in the first place, then you simply need to provide evidence to future employers that you still have such virtues and will bring them to bear in your future work too. A common interview question relates to this so we will present it to you as Activity 7.3.

ACTIVITY 7.3   EXEMPLARS OF PERSEVERANCE

Thinking back over recent years, provide an example of a situation in which you faced problems in achieving a work-related goal but surmounted them. What kept you going in those circumstances?

Keep a note of minor as well as major triumphs such as these and the tactics you used to achieve them. These will come in useful for your 'records of achievement' discussed in Chapter 8.

Ensuring social and political survival

One of the key areas of 'soft skills' is the art of working with others. Where there are people, there will be decisions to be made on all kinds of things, such as whose turn it is to make the tea, and there will be compromises to be negotiated, for instance how resources are allocated and to whom, etc. This means all working environments are both social and political. Where social survival might be concerned with learning to successfully navigate your working environment, it could be said that successful political survival develops with experience. Both are unavoidable but you can persist by being the best you can be in your professional role, by being fair and consistent in your conduct, and by treating others as you would like to be treated.

You can achieve a good measure of social survival by paying attention to some basic matters, including: the local dress code, your personal hygiene, table manners, being polite and courteous, and by being respectful of and to colleagues and your organisation in all ways, including in person, in writing and online, and even at interviews with other organisations! Challenge any bad behaviour you may witness or experience and be assertive, rather than aggressive, if people treat you or your colleagues in a way you think inappropriate. You should remain true to yourself, without your heart or your anger taking over, considering that other important attribute, integrity. Seek out techniques for being:

- adaptable;
- flexible;
- assertive.

Politics might be about compromise, but it is also about power, and the use thereof, which can be a positive and negative force in the workplace. Lobbying is a useful way of disseminating ideas and garnering support if you are trying to influence those with the power to make decisions, or who allocate budgets. Gossiping, on the other hand, is not a good tactic. There can be considerable negative power in gossiping, where members of a group decide who is 'in' and 'out' and in what way. Both lobbying and gossiping share a fine line with networking (especially gossiping in its 'heard it on the grapevine' sense); they all provide useful mechanisms for sourcing both information and mis-information.

Employers, including academic employers, are looking for employees who understand the business they are in and who can use this knowledge to think strategically, spot trends and drive ideas/developments forward. This is being political in the broader, more positive sense. You will not be able to think strategically or influence outcomes unless you understand the way your organisation works and the context in which the business operates. Taking a broader interest in events that impact on you and your research area is one way of beginning to develop your 'business' knowledge.

Team working

Teams are groups of people who work together on a shared project, objectives or tasks; they may exist on a long term or short term basis. The success of the team will depend on how well the members work together, so there has been considerable interest in the composition of successful teams and the types of people who make up their membership, with Meredith Belbin's work perhaps the most well-known in this area (see Belbin 1981 in ideas for further reading, below). Advances in technology coupled with competitive economic demands mean that employers require a flexible and adaptable workforce, or people who can apply their expertise in versatile ways, working alongside and with a range of others.

Good team players put the needs of the team before their personal interests and are committed to the aims of the team. Team players will work in open and transparent ways, and be supportive of their colleagues. Being mindful that different people possess different qualities and attributes, and bring different gifts to the group, it is important that you identify what your contributions are.

Researchers in STEMM areas may have greater opportunity to work in teams than those in HASS, but everyone has the possibility to get involved with a team socially (through sport or a hobby) or as a volunteer. Researchers can use these opportunities and experiences to reflect on their own team-working style and range of contributions.

REFLECTION POINT

Think of a good colleague or team member you know and consider what makes them stand out for you? What do they do? How do they behave? And what qualities do they exhibit to make them outstanding? Consider how your qualities might be viewed by your colleagues.

Working collaboratively

Collegiality is an important concept in academia, alongside team work, because of the need to support the notion of respect for independence of thought and intellectual property. When the need for refinement of ideas through challenge and debate is considered, it is clear that, while it is important to have your ideas contested, without collegiality you would not be able to trust revealing publically your more outrageous but potentially fruitful inspirations. Thus, despite competition within the discipline and between institutions for scarce resources and for acclaim, it is essential that researchers collaborate to help each other. Collaboration is necessary also to:

- solve complex puzzles;
- profit from constructive, critical feedback;
- provide a collective, authoritative voice;
- benefit from experience and expertise;
- make the most efficient and economic use of rare or expensive equipment and materials;
- recognise joint responsibilities;
- provide advice and support to those with less experience.

None of those things can be achieved without a sense of basic trust in and respect for colleagues, be they working on a project with you, working on similar issues in your discipline or other disciplines, in your region, country or another land. They may be working in academia or in industry, be a formal team member in close proximity or part of a diffuse, international drive to explore and solve a certain problem.

It is actually very heartening and inspiring to know that you are part of a community of scholars, willing to ask for and consider advice or give it freely, and with whom to share joys and frustrations. To become part of that community, we each must demonstrate a whole range of skills, including a willingness to ask for support when it is needed, listen to advice and give it due consideration, communicate requests and advice effectively, and, perhaps the most important, be humble and tolerant of others. These are all of the qualities that also underpin team working.

There are few research projects nowadays that can be conducted in isolation. Even the individual contribution to knowledge required of doctoral researchers requires liaison with supervisors, librarians, trainers and so on, while post-doctoral researchers will have a principal investigator, other colleagues such as technicians and a range of stakeholders, including funders, to work with. Each person, no matter what their status, is expected to contribute to the final output of the research, though some may make a small contribution while others provide a substantial one; some may contribute in person and others from a distance. So collaboration involves skills of recognising the importance of others' contributions, of balancing contributions and using a range of communication skills. This is where your networking skills (see Chapter 6) really come in useful as you build up partnerships with people from a range of backgrounds to stimulate understanding of and from different perspectives.

By now we hope to have convinced you of the interrelation between skills and the need to be able to convince others that you have them. We will develop the latter idea further in the next chapter.

Ideas for further reading

Diversity

Equality Challenge Unit has useful advice and information on their website at: www.ecu. ac.uk/ (retrieved 8/4/2013).

Vitae: *Every Researcher Counts: Equality and Diversity in Researcher Careers in HEIs*: www.vitae. ac.uk/everyresearchercounts (retrieved 25/09/2013).

Leadership and management

ACAS (2009) *Advisory Booklet – Managing Conflict at Work*. Available online at: www.acas. org.uk/index.aspx?articleid=1218 (retrieved 22/4/2013).

Autry, J.A. (2001) *The Servant Leader*. Roseville, CA: Prima Publishing.

Blanchard, K. *The One Minute Manager* series and audio CDs. London: HarperCollins.

Drucker, P.F. (1973) *Management: Tasks – Responsibilities – Practices*. New York: Harper Collins.

Johnson, S. and McGregor, H. (2005) 'Recognizing and supporting a scholarship of practice: Soft skills are hard!', *Asia-Pacific Journal of Cooperative Education* 6(1): 1–6.

A useful insight for engineers.

Radcliffe, S. (2012) *Leadership – Plain and Simple* (2nd edition). Harlow: Pearson Education. Also see Steve's website and blog at: www.futureengagedeliver.com/ (retrieved 20/4/2013).

Zenger, J.H. and Folkman, J.R. (2009) *The Extraordinary Leader: Turning Good Managers into Great Leaders*. New York: McGraw-Hill.

Personal effectiveness

Covey, S. (1989) *The 7 Habits of Highly Effective People: Powerful Lessons in Personal Change*. London: Simon & Schuster.

Denicolo, P. and Becker, L. (2012) *Developing Research Proposals*. London: Sage.

Klaus, P. (2007) *The Hard Truth about Soft Skills: Workplace Lessons Smart People Wished They'd Learned Sooner*. New York: Harper Collins.

Ted Talks: 'Riveting talks by remarkable people, free to the world'. Available at: www.ted. com/.

Social and political survival

Rozakis, L. and Rozakis, B. (1998) *The Complete Idiot's Guide to Office Politics*. New York: Alpha Books.

Robert Whipple's *14 Rules for Political Survival (soon to be 15)*: http://leadergrow.com/ articles/47-ideas-for-political-survival (retrieved 2/12/2012).

Team working

Belbin, R.M. (1981) *Management Teams: Why They Succeed or Fail.* Oxford: Butterworth-Heinemann.

Fleming, I. (2004) *The Teamworking Pocketbook* (2nd edition). Arlesford, UK: Management Pocketbooks Ltd.

8

HOW CAN SKILL DEVELOPMENT BE EVIDENCED, ASSESSED AND EVALUATED?

Chapter overview

This chapter discusses:

- Assessment
- Evaluation
- Evidence
- Performance reviews/appraisals
- Professional development plans (PDP)
- Portfolios
- Return on investment (ROI)

Introduction

Monitoring your progress is essential for ensuring that you are developing as a professional. There may be some formal mechanisms that you are subject to as a researcher, for example an annual or other form of periodic review, up-grade/transfer or confirmation process as a doctoral researcher, and a probationary period and annual appraisal as postdoctoral staff. All of these mechanisms help to monitor project progress and your performance. Outside these formal mechanisms, an institution may operate interim monitoring systems for researchers. Doctoral researchers will have regular meetings with their supervisor(s), and research staff with their PI, but these meetings may focus exclusively on the progress of the research rather than your professional development and performance as an individual. We recommend that you seek a regular review of your professional development if it is not already part of the process. You may have captured your starting point or benchmarked your skill level in a TNA/LNA/DNA (see Chapter 2), and then monitored and reviewed your progress throughout, but if not, it would be sensible to start now. A range of methods for monitoring progress are discussed below.

Assessment

As an undergraduate it was quite likely that your work was always being assessed and marked in some way, that is you were measured against a 'learning outcome' which would have been written into your course or programme. A lot of these mechanisms would have served a two-fold purpose: first, to provide the student with an idea of how well they were performing; and second, to assure the course convenor that the course was achieving what it set out to do. The latter aspect of the assessment process would form part of a wider quality assurance process that would determine if the 'product' (education/programme/course) was meeting the required standards and expectations. However, as you become more independent as a researcher, so the formal mechanisms for assessing your progress change and even diminish. While formal doctoral assessment comes in the form of the viva voce (the oral defence of your work), waiting several years to know whether you are on the right track and your research has reached the recognised standard is a high-risk approach, so it is likely that other kinds of assessment will take place throughout your degree programme, as described above. This 'quality assurance' mechanism determines if the research project and the candidate are capable of meeting the doctoral standard.

There is very little formal assessment of ECRs other than job performance reviews during the probationary period and annual appraisals. Excepting the Research Excellence Framework (REF) (UK), unless you are studying for a formal qualification, such as a teaching qualification, you will probably not have your work formally assessed and marked. It is therefore, arguably, a general law of professional development that the higher up the ladder you progress, the more likely it is that you have to create your own assessment structures and quality assure your own progress for making effective reports to seniors in appraisals (see below).

For monitoring the progress of professional development, such as whether your communication skills have improved, other mechanisms will be necessary. You could begin by setting some clear objectives within a timeframe and using the 'SMART' tool (see Chapter 6) to help you achieve your goals, for example improving your presentation or people management skills. Such objectives help both to maintain your motivation by ensuring you have something to aim for and to monitor your progress against. These objectives would form part of a Professional/Personal Development Plan (PDP) and once achieved should be recorded as evidence of development and could form part of a portfolio or record of achievement, described below.

There are a number of other ways to assess your skills, including assessment of your strengths and weaknesses, and whether you have achieved the appropriate standard or level for your stage of development. You could ask for feedback from peers, supervisors, colleagues, and students, known formally as 360 degree feedback. There is much you can learn from this powerful mechanism – if everyone is honest, open and constructive and willing to listen. You could use a skills matrix to position yourself; currently the most useful one for researchers in the UK is the Vitae RDF. Further, you could look to another professional body for insight into its assessment criteria and method; this would be especially useful if you planned to work in that specific professional area. For example, for teaching, the Higher Education Academy's Professional Standards Framework (HEA PSF) would be useful. Professional bodies may offer the opportunity for formal recognition and accreditation of meeting a standard. The most common form of accreditation within institutions is a teaching qualification, which you may be able to access as a doctoral candidate, but it is worth asking what else might be available to you either in your institution or in your subject area. Often accreditation can be achieved via the submission of a portfolio of evidence, such as with the Chartered Institute of Personnel and Development, which may suit the busy lifestyle of researchers better.

Evaluation

There is much debate over the difference between assessment and evaluation. Generally speaking, assessment confirms improvement, provides feedback and pushes the forming process along, whereas evaluation makes judgements about the quality and 'the sum' of the process, such as whether or not expected outcomes have been achieved. In development terms, however, it allows for reflection on the process of learning itself and what might need to be done in the future.

It is highly likely that, at some point, you have been asked to evaluate courses you have attended. For example, what was most useful or least useful in the course, how would you rate the skills of the presenter, etc. This form of observation will have captured your immediate thoughts, feelings and perceptions at the end of a process or course. More sophisticated methods will ask you to write a reflective statement, perhaps about what you hope to get out of the course/programme (pre-event) and what you found useful after the event. This form of evaluation is useful for making you think about what you are doing and why you wanted to attend the course in the first instance, but on the whole these kinds of evaluation are about rating your *reaction* to the event itself and what, if anything, you can remember or will put to use later. This is all vital information for trainers and programme designers but they do not, by themselves, provide evidence of *your* development.

Even those evaluation processes that return several months later to find out what you have learned and applied in the workplace will largely be indicating to the training provider that the course was worth putting on. Although this more thorough evaluation may capture any change or improvement in your performance, and check whether you met your objectives or the objectives set for you, it commonly does so from the trainer's perspective rather than yours as the learner or participant. What is missing in this process (and where there is no existing mechanism to close the 'learning loop' for individuals) is your own appreciation and understanding of how well you are improving or progressing professionally or, better still, an independent perspective on your progression.

As an up-coming professional you should be interested in three things and they all require evaluation: (i) the extent of learning and the personal change you are experiencing, (ii) the standard at which you are performing or operating and (iii) how much value you are adding to your discipline/department or organisation. The first two apply to all researchers, whereas the last applies especially to research staff and therefore it is important for ECRs to evaluate their skill base and level of performance if they want to pursue a career in academia. Careful consideration of what is required for a specific stage of development must be entered into, using guidance and advice from supervisors/PIs, mentors, colleagues and external professional frameworks such as the HEA PSF and Vitae RDF, and job descriptions. Different phases of skill development are needed at different points in a career, that is from basic and introductory to more practised and advanced levels, and beyond this to a considerable level of mastery. Therefore you should be continuously assessing and evaluating your needs, your improvements and achievements and your progress to ensure you are moving forward to meet the recognised standard for your career stage.

An obvious evaluation tool is the RDF whereby you can initially identify where you are within each descriptor, select several you would like to improve on over the forthcoming year, and review your overall position and progress in the chosen descriptors regularly, certainly annually. You can also look at job descriptions, especially for the next role you aspire to, even if that is two to three years away. These will give you an insight into what is required and how you measure up. This is not only useful for initial TNA/DNA/LNA (Chapter 2), but also for measuring your progress against to see if you are ready to apply for that lectureship or management role. We have noted a range of evaluation models in Box 8.1 and suggest a simple self-evaluation task in Activity 8.1.

BOX 8.1   MODELS OF EVALUATION

The common aim for these models is to capture the impact of a training intervention in a qualitative and transformative sense. A digest of each is provided for you to follow up.

- Donald Kirkpatrick's four-level training programme evaluation is perhaps the most famous evaluation model (Kirkpatrick 2006):
  - Level 1 – reactions of participant to the event.
  - Level 2 – learning; for example, has there been an increase in knowledge or capability?
  - Level 3 – behaviour; have there been any demonstrable improvements or changes in behaviour?
  - Level 4 – results; this will seek to capture the effects on the 'business', that is, your discipline, department, university, organisation or society.
- CIRO model: Context, Input, Reaction and Outcome (Warr et al. 1970). Broader than Kirkpatrick's model and less arduous in terms of separating learning from behavioural change.
- The Ripple model of *satisfaction*, *learning*, *change*, *value* is based on Phil Race's view of how people learn and also has four levels of evaluation (see www2.rgu.ac.uk/celt/pgcerttlt/how/how4d.htm (retrieved 18/07/13) and Race (1993) at the end of this chapter).

  - Needing/Wanting – the motivation of the participant to learn.
  - Doing – practice, including trial and error.
  - Feedback – seeing the results, as evidenced in other people's reactions.
  - Digesting – making sense of it and gaining ownership.

- UK Impact (and evaluation) Framework. This model is based on Kirkpatrick and is the framework HEIs are applying to assess researcher development in the UK.
- 'Plan – do – review' from Vitae's *The Leading Researcher* (2011: 9). This is, perhaps, the most user-friendly version for researchers' self-evaluation. It consists of a simple 'plan – do – review' approach that is easily applied to any situation.

ACTIVITY 8.1   COURSE ATTENDANCE PERSONAL EVALUATION

When embarking on a training course, look at the learning outcomes for the course and list them in a table, as below. Detail how you think you will apply each outcome in your work. Then assess your level of confidence in each area before and after the course.

Learning outcome:	How will you apply this outcome in your work?	Rate your current level of confidence against each outcome from 1 to 5 (where 1 is little or no confidence and 5 is extremely confident)	Post-course review – rate your confidence again
A	X	2	
B	Y	1	

You could ask your supervisor/PI if they have noticed any changes in your performance or behaviour; for instance, can they confirm that you are applying the outcomes in the workplace?

A note of caution here: it is quite common for people to rate themselves higher *before* a training intervention than afterwards! The apparent regression in skill level is attributed not to a lack of learning or inferior training experience (although that is possible), but to the experience resulting in a more realistic appraisal of actual level of competency, illustrating the move from 'unconscious incompetence' to 'conscious incompetence'. The 'conscious competence' theory of learning is the final evaluative method researchers might find useful to think about. It suggests that a learner moves through the four stages: unconscious incompetence, conscious incompetence, conscious competence, to unconscious competence (where one can do something automatically).

Evidence

Just as you must provide evidence to back up assertions in a research report, so you must for your professional development. Completing one research project does not, of itself, prove you can manage any other; you need to convince a future employer of your transferable skills. For instance, you could provide examples that demonstrate both your understanding of project management models and tools and that your capabilities exist at a certain level. Certificates of qualifications or course attendance provide evidence of learning/skill acquisition at a minimum level but you need to provide evidence of how you applied that skill in your work. In our example this might be illustrated by detail about how you managed and monitored that project, how you anticipated change, and how you responded to any problems the project faced. Prospective employers want to know what *you* did and what *you* have learned, as this is how they can assess the extent to which you (as compared with other candidates) might add value to their department. You would be demonstrating a good deal of learning if you described the strengths and weaknesses of the methods you used, their advantages and disadvantages, and what you would do differently next time. All of the above would make you sound more credible and plausible as a project manager than someone who simply pointed to their thesis and assumed that their skill in this area was self-evident. The strength and credibility of your evidence really counts when employers are choosing between candidates.

It is good practice to use different examples to illustrate different attributes and experiences, rather than relying solely on your first main project. Think this through carefully, especially for application forms and interviews. You will need to find a variety of examples to demonstrate your range of skills. This means you may need to draw on activity beyond your research to provide evidence of what you are able to do. Trust us – you will probably have lots of these examples. Do not be afraid to cite voluntary work, sports activities, a seminar you organised for your peers or the small grant you applied for. They all count. At a deeper level, it is advantageous to provide explicit examples of when you used the skill or applied new knowledge in settings other than the obvious research ones since this will signify the transfer of learning from one setting to another.

Portfolios, e-portfolios, logs, records of achievement, 'super CV' (see Chapter 9) or just a list of your activities, are all examples of how you might keep track of your achievements and what you have done and learnt. In addition, Human Resources at the Massachusetts Institute of Technology (MIT) have a great skills exercise which asks for examples of when a skill was used. We accessed it online at: http://hrweb.mit.edu/system/files/Skills+Exercise.pdf. This might be a good time to engage in Activity 8.2.

ACTIVITY 8.2   PROVIDING EVIDENCE

What evidence can you provide for changes in the following areas?

- A level in a specific skill
- New knowledge you have gained
- An attitude relevant to your work
- Your behaviour relevant in the workplace
- Your professional and working relationships – have you extended your network, created new collaborative partners?
- The quality of your research work – are you performing to a higher standard, working more efficiently?

Would these changes indicate that you are ready for promotion? Do you know the criteria being applied? If not, find out so that you provide the most appropriate evidence.

Performance reviews

The performance review or appraisal is the institution's or line manager's way of assessing your performance over a given period, usually annually. Appraisals look at your performance and if you have not had one as a postdoc you must ask for one because it will assist with your career development. Annual appraisals are applied in different ways. Some have pro-forma that an organisation uses to design future training programmes with. For instance, if everyone needed to use Twitter in their job and recorded on their appraisal form that they were unable to tweet, the organisation's response should be to find a way of addressing this development need for the staff. This would be an example of best practice but you may find that you not only need to self-assess your skill level, but also generate your own training needs response. An enterprising researcher might even design their own appraisal form and ask their supervisor or PI to assess them against it – and we know researchers who have done just this!

ACTIVITY 8.3   DESIGN YOUR OWN APPRAISAL SYSTEM

What criteria would you like to be assessed against? Publications and funding applications are obvious areas, but what other development would benefit your:

(Continued)

(Continued)

career development?

next job application?

personal development?

Set out your criteria in a table like the one for Activity 8.1 and ask for your current performance to be rated.

Professional development plans (PDPs)

Let us return to the swimming analogy we encountered in Chapter 1. Imagine you are swimming the English Channel, for example. You leave the shore and begin swimming with great enthusiasm, but after a couple of hours swimming you may begin to wonder how far you have swum and how much further you have yet to swim. At this point your enthusiasm may wane as you confront the expanse of water before you. However, if you regularly stop swimming, tread water, turn round and look back to the shore, you can assess and reflect on the distance you have travelled rather than focus on what is left to do. This will enable you to set little targets for where you would like to be when you next review your position and provides you with the opportunity to congratulate yourself on how far you have come. This is the essence of PDP and it is a vital method for keeping your career and/or professional development on track, especially if you are in a profession that is mainly concerned with outputs and products, such as thesis production and publications, and in which projects take years to complete.

PDP involves having an overall plan or goal, and a clear idea of what you need to do or would like to achieve in the time that stands between you now and your future goal. Break that time down into years (if appropriate) and the year ahead into months or weeks even; this begins to put a structure around your overall plan/goal. Populate the plan with the details of what needs to be done and with key milestones, perhaps every four or five weeks, and/or deliverables along the way. In short, this is applying the principles of project management to your self-development! A review should take no more than an hour of your time – but regularity is essential. It will remind you of where you are headed and what you want to achieve and give you a realistic assessment (formative) of whether or not you will achieve the end result.

Whatever profession you aspire to, you would need to know what the job entails and self-assess yourself to see if you met the criteria. The internet and online application processes make it easier to access criteria in job descriptions and person specifications. If you do not meet the criteria, you can build the development of the areas you have identified for improvement into your PDP and work on this as you move towards your goal(s). Once a goal has been obtained, you can set new goals and draw up new plans. The PDP is a living and ongoing document, and useful for enabling you achieve longer term objectives such as those researchers face, for instance obtaining a doctorate or securing a permanent post. The key to PDP lies in *knowing*, *planning* and *reviewing*: knowing what you want and planning how to get there, and reviewing your progress towards achieving it.

Professional people use PDPs to plan their career progression because no one else will do this for them at their level of expertise. Indeed, this (in conjunction with coaching) is a major tool among professional staff. Your career master plan might extend 10–15 years ahead, but the timeframe really depends on what you can deal with. However, *everyone* should be planning their career 3–5 years ahead, rather than only looking for the next job and its requirements when your contract is due to run out or your thesis has been submitted. Smart and talented people should be looking at least two roles ahead.

Portfolios

Researchers in the Arts and Humanities will be familiar with the idea of a portfolio, where maintaining a collection of work (documents, art, textiles, images, videos, etc.) that showcase an individual's talent and ideas is common practice. The principles of the portfolio are exactly the same for researchers in other disciplinary areas, that is, to maintain a collection of the best documents/images/evidence to showcase your achievements, work and talent. They can take the form of elaborate learning logs, debriefing reports, teaching evaluations, feedback from examiners or a simple collection of records of achievement, which build into a book or file. Portfolios can be substantive, as is the case with a paper record of achievement, or abstract as contained in the notion of a 'portfolio career' where one builds on a range of skills and achievements to move from one role to another.

In substantive terms, your portfolio should certainly contain any certificates you may have and testimonials you have received and/or informal as well as formal feedback. You can keep it as a CV, as a paper file or booklet, or go public with it online as a webpage or blog. Indeed, Facebook and LinkedIn, for example, provide web space that is based on a portfolio type of approach. There are a variety of e-portfolio packages available (Pebblepad is common in education), but you need to find the scheme that suits your needs. There is no point having an elaborate online system if you never fill it in or keep it up; experiment to see what works best for you.

Return on investment (ROI)

A tougher form of the evaluation question is 'what is the return on investment (ROI)?' This can be measured in terms of research outputs, money, publications, collaborations, new projects generated, etc., and ultimately in the UK by the Research Excellence Framework (REF). Sometimes developers prefer to measure the return on expectation (ROE) to the ROI but, if money is being spent, organisations will want to see tangible outcomes and financial benefits, usually in quantifiable terms. The concept of ROI is not common among HEIs but is creeping into the discourse of some areas. You do not have to look for huge financial gains; even modest improvements in performance can be translated into time saved, which in turn can be calculated in terms of hourly pay and totalled in financial terms. Clearly this approach is more pertinent to ECRs than PGRs. However, even if you do not have an official hourly rate you could give yourself a hypothetical one and calculate improvements or financial savings on that basis. There are lots of different ways of producing ROI, but you cannot assess any level of improvement or calculate any returns unless you know where you started from, that is, your benchmark or baseline.

If financial returns are not your style, you could think about measuring gains against your expectations: what did you expect to improve as a result of an activity and by how much? You might expect an improvement in your written text if you attend a writing course, but if the course was more about writing style than the correct use of grammar then your expectations may not have been met. Thus it is important that you are clear about your needs and identify them specifically (as discussed in Chapter 2) and that you select the right form and level of intervention (as discussed in Chapter 3) so that you can then assess the impact the intervention has made and, beyond this, how it met expectations or produced an outcome for the investment of time and effort. There is a good deal of overlap between a ROI analysis and the academic interest in the impact of research. By considering the impact of your research you will be using an approach similar to ROI.

REFLECTION POINT

How much have you grown as a professional in the last year? Where would you like to be in a year's time? What do you need to improve to get there and how will you know you have succeeded?

What everyone wants to know

The fundamental issue and what everyone needs to know, including you, research funders, employers, universities, developers, supervisors, PIs, etc. is this: have the training or development activities made any difference?

There are two key things development should achieve: the first is recognisable learning and the second is the application of that learning in your working environment, often known as learning or workplace transfer. As a researcher you will already be using methods for capturing learning and reflecting on the outcome of events. Scientists and engineers will be familiar with applying debrief techniques, as will some qualitative researchers. Researchers in HASS may be more used to reflective techniques. Whichever technique you prefer, the key issue is to be conscious of what difference the experience or intervention made to you, how it has impacted on your professional growth, and how you have applied (transferred) the learning to your working environment and practice. Try the After Action Review below in Activity 8.4.

ACTIVITY 8.4 AFTER ACTION REVIEW (AAR)

This is a short, sharp and non-judgemental approach to learning that was initially created by the US Army. Debriefing has a long history in the armed services and this is a tool for rapid reflection and post-event learning. It should last no more than 30 minutes and include all the relevant participants, but you can go through the questioning process by yourself. The key to success is an open and honest response, comparing what was intended (or expected) with what actually happened.

Apply the following questions to an event you organise or next attend:

1. What was supposed to happen?
2. What did happen?

(Continued)

(Continued)

3. Why was there a difference?
4. What can I/we learn from this? How do I/we capture this and take it forward?

Considering what you learned, what will you use in the future and do differently next time? This last point is critical – it is *the* development question. It provides the means for deconstructing your actions and providing yourself with the basis for improvement.

If you are unable to self-assess, ask your colleagues, supervisor or PI for feedback or to discuss the event with you.

Ideas for further reading

Denney, F., Mead, J., Toombs, P. (2011) *The Leading Researcher*. Cambridge: Careers Research and Advisory Centre (CRAC) Limited. Available online from Vitae at: http://www.vitae.ac.uk/researcherbooklets (retrieved 25/09/2013).

Kirkpatrick, J.D. (2006) *Evaluating Training Programs: The Four Levels* (3rd edition). San Francisco, CA: Berrett-Koehler.

Race, P. (2005) *Making Learning Happen: A Guide for Post-compulsory Education*. London: Sage.

Rae, L. (1999) *Using Evaluation in Training and Development*. London: Kogan Page.

Vitae, *The Impact Framework 2012*. Available at: www.vitae.ac.uk/impactframework (retrieved 25/09/2013).

Warr, P.B., Bird, M. and Rackham, N. (1970) *The Evaluation of Management Training*. Aldershot: Gower.

See the Business Balls website at: www.businessballs.com/trainingprogramevaluation.htm (retrieved 4/4/2013).

9

HOW CAN TRANSFERABLE SKILLS BE MARKETED EFFECTIVELY TO ENHANCE EMPLOYABILITY?

Chapter overview

This chapter, contributed by Dr Dawn Duke, addresses:

- Effective communication with a range of audiences within and outside the academy
- Common mistakes and how to avoid them
- Demonstration of skills in CVs and interviews

Marketing your skills, especially your transferable skills, is essential for building networks and opening up opportunities. The key to success lies primarily in how you communicate your skills, experience and research to others. You will need to be able to identify what your specific audience cares about and adapt your communication technique to suit each unique situation. It is a matter of tailoring your message so that it best resonates with your target audience. This chapter will discuss how to develop the skills necessary to market yourself and then will provide ideas and tips to help you promote your skills effectively, allowing you to open up a range of interesting possibilities for yourself.

Bridging the gap between your research world and that of a wider audience

The first step to employability is to be able to communicate clearly with a broad range of people. All professions will require you to work with a wide range of people, so you will be expected to express yourself effectively to people of a variety of backgrounds. This is true for both academic and non-academic jobs. Therefore, the first step in successfully marketing yourself to employers is to learn how to share your research and your skills to a broader audience. To do this it is helpful to take a step back and look at your research in a slightly different way. Normally researchers spend a lot of time thinking about and justifying 'how' they are going to do things. We as researchers naturally focus on the details of research to make complex decisions about how the research should proceed. However, broader, lay audiences care a lot less about the 'hows' and much more about the 'whys' and the 'so whats'. A broader audience does not want to be taught the details of your field or your research methodology. They want to know about the big picture, why your research is important, but particularly, why is it important to *them*. They want to know what impact your research is going to have on the world, especially the world on their doorstep.

One major thing to watch out for in your explanations to them is jargon. Jargon is technical language that we use within a particular field to describe complex and often abstract concepts. Researchers are not the only ones who use jargon; in fact most professions do. You may well have gone to the garage to have your car fixed and have a mechanic talk to you in a manner that baffles you with jargon about crankshafts and catalytic converters. How did that make you feel? Most of us feel highly suspicious of someone when they talk to us in this way. That is not how you wish to make your audience feel. Therefore, it is important to learn to translate jargon into language that is understandable to everyone. See Box 9.1 for some ideas to help you avoid 'blinding your audience with science' and then try Activity 9.1 to develop your skill through practice.

BOX 9.1   JARGON BUSTING TIPS

'Making things complicated is simple; making things simple is very complicated!' (PhD student in Geography)
'The art of good teaching is to make the arcane accessible.' (PhD Supervisor)

1. **Translation**: Some words just need a simple translation. Sometimes the translation does not feel exactly 'right' to you as a researcher in your field, but if it gets the message across, it really does not matter. For example, I used to struggle to explain 'gene expression' to people outside of my field, until I realised I could translate it to 'gene activity'.
2. **Analogy, metaphor or short stories**: When simple translation does not work, it can be helpful to compare your complex concept to something that people are generally

familiar with or to tell them a bit of a story to help them understand the significance. In biology, the brain has been described as a telephone exchange or, more recently, as a computer. In physics, the structure of an atom has been illustrated as a planetary system. These are not exact models, of course, but they illustrate key points that the scientist wants to convey.

3. **Use models/drawing/physical descriptions**: Some concepts are much easier to understand visually than through words. Pictures truly can be worth 1,000 words.

4. **Leave it out**: Remember, they do not need to know all of the details of your field. Leave out as much of the technical detail as possible. Focus on what is truly important to THEM, what difference will it make to their lives.

ACTIVITY 9.1 WHAT IS YOUR BIG PICTURE?

Find a friend who is not in your research field and explain to them why your research is important. What is the big picture problem you are investigating? How have (or will) your findings move your field forward? How might it (eventually) contribute to society, even if only a little bit? Consider next how you would explain this to your grandparents, to a reporter from your local newspaper, and then to an editor from a professional journal in your field. Think of how you would change what you would emphasise and what words you would use for each of these different audiences.

Improving your ability to talk with others about your research will greatly enhance your ability to perform well in an interview situation. Practise talking to a broad range of people about your research. Ask them what they find most interesting or important about what you do. They may surprise you with their different perspectives. Learning to be able to tailor your message for particular audience, being sensitive to what they care about, will not only help you market your skills, but will also enable you create networks and potential collaborations.

Know your audience

The first step in tailoring your message requires some research to answer some questions: Who is your target audience? What do they know about the world of research? What are they looking for in an employee? These are very important questions because without understanding your audience you are unlikely to be able to communicate effectively with them. For the purpose of marketing yourself to employers, we will divide your audience into two groups: (1) academic employers and (2) non-academic employers.

Academic employers

Most researchers feel they understand the world of academia. By the time you have achieved your doctorate you have spent much of your life within this environment. You have learned to communicate using an academic style while writing your thesis and perhaps peer-reviewed publications; you have presented to academic communities within your department and, most likely, beyond, and you think you speak the same language (remember, though, the quotation, variously attributed but most frequently to George Bernard Shaw, about Britain and the USA being two countries divided by a common language!). By and large, academics do understand what your doctorate and other research experience generally entailed, although there may well be people on an interview or selection panel from other disciplines or from human resources who are unfamiliar with your specific subject or the details of your experience. Even though the audience may seem familiar, since you have been interacting with people within academia for years, when they are recruiting for positions there are some specific qualities they are looking for. These qualities are in fact quite similar to those on any other employer; it is just the context of them that is different. Below is a list of three common mistakes people make when applying for an academic post, each with suggestions about how to avoid or circumvent them.

Mistake #1: Being too focused on the past

When interviewing for most academic positions, it is quite common to give a presentation about your research. The most common mistake we see researchers make in this presentation is to focus almost entirely on their past research. This is understandable because this is the style of research presentation that you are used to making at seminars or conferences. You talk about what you have done. However, an interview calls for a different type of presentation. This audience cares much more about what you *can* do than what you *have* done. Obviously, these two things are related, as what you have done in the past gives a demonstration of your skills and abilities. However, a typical research presentation does not give your audience the full story about what you could bring to the new position.

The main emphasis of an academic interview presentation should stress how you will fit into the research environment at the university to which you are applying. Every university is different, as is every faculty, department and research group. How will you fit into their research strategy? Will you be able to collaborate with different members of the university? Your talk should emphasise not only what you can do, but also clearly show how this will fit in with other research that is already established within the university. You should show that you have done some research about their interest, context, previous successes, and so on.

It is also extremely important to show that you have plans for future research, as well as showing that you have an idea about how you will fund and disseminate it. If you are being interviewed for a research fellow position, discuss how your past research can be used within the context of this new research group to bring a new dimension to their research. If you are applying for a lectureship, indicate the direction you see your research taking in the future. Also discuss how you plan to get the publications and funding you will need to be successful in this future post.

Mistake #2: Looking like everyone else

When applying for a post in academia, it is safe to assume the other candidates will also have a doctorate in a similar area to you. What makes you different? This is a key message to communicate. What can you do that others may not be able to? The answer to this question often lies in the unique combination of learning experiences you have had. Think of the full range of what you can offer – your research skills along with your transferable skills. The next step is to link this skill set and experience to the position you are applying for and build a case about how you are perfectly suited for this job, which will develop in a unique way with your input.

Mistake #3: Forgetting about or downplaying your transferable skills

It is very easy to become focused on research skills when applying for jobs in academia. Often academic positions ask for specific research techniques, or certain numbers of publications, or maybe even previous grants. If you do not actually meet these specifications you may feel you do not have a chance of getting the position. However, by demonstrating that you have the skills necessary to meet these criteria in the near future, you may well win over your audience. This is where your wider skills come in. Knowing a certain technique or method is a basic research skill, demonstrating that you are versatile, having the ability to effectively master new research techniques, is a highly valuable transferable skill in academia. Therefore, demonstrating this transferable skill can make up for not knowing a specific research skill.

Likewise, if you do not have the publications you need yet, you can demonstrate you have the necessary skills in written communication as well as an understanding of the strategic planning necessary to turn your current results into good publications. You could draw up in advance abstracts or outlines of prospective journal articles, with a list of intended and appropriate journals to which you propose to submit them, to demonstrate your potential even if you have not yet had time to write the full article and get it published. Doing this will not waste your time because, even if you are not offered that particular job, you have begun the preparation to improve your CV. (See another book in this Success in Research Series that will help: *Publishing Journal Articles*.)

Securing grant funding requires an understanding of the research climate in your field and the ability to target the funding streams that are most likely to support your research. Furthermore, you have to demonstrate the ability to build a strong case for support. If you can convince the interview panel that you have these skills (evidence, even, of small funding applications will help), they are more likely to believe you have what it takes to be able to be a success in your new position. As above, you can prepare in advance an outline of what you will, in the future, seek funding for and from whom. (See another book in this Success in Research Series that will help: *Developing Research Proposals*.) Showing you have these necessary professional skills is critical.

Non-academic employers

More and more researchers are being employed outside academia. This is due to a combination of increased numbers of people pursuing doctorates, a reduction in the jobs available within academia along with increased demand for highly skilled people in the private sector, and the need for professionals of many kinds to develop research skills to further their careers. John Watkins, Head of University of Surrey's Career's Service observes: 'Employers are increasingly seeking that little bit extra from those emerging from university. Postgraduate researchers are often well placed to be able to demonstrate these skills from both an academic and practical perspective.'

However, taking advantage of job opportunities beyond academia can be a challenge, especially for those who have spent their entire career thus far within the academy. If you have never worked outside academia, you may find this audience a bit harder to communicate with. Many researchers live duel lives of sorts; they talk about research at the university, but when they go home they avoid talking to others about their work as much as possible.

To start this task of marketing yourself to non-academic audiences it is important to understand what they know and do not know about research and researchers (and perhaps what they think they know which may be wrong). Activity 9.2 is a simple exercise to learn a bit more about what people outside academia think about researchers.

ACTIVITY 9.2   UNDERSTANDING A NON-ACADEMIC POINT OF VIEW

Ask five people, from a variety of backgrounds, who have not done a doctorate, the following questions:
- What do they think PGRs do?
- What do they think researchers or lecturers within the university do?
- What do they think is the skill set these researchers have?
- Consider how those answers compare to your own responses to these questions.

What you are likely to find through this activity is that most people think the doctorate concerns learning a particular subject in even more detail, and about becoming more focused and narrow. People often think a doctorate is an extension of undergraduate or master's education, where you are guided and directed to 'learn more stuff', and become yet narrower in your area of expertise and probably becoming very 'intellectual' and divorced from the 'real' world. In the first paragraph of 'An employer's perspective' in Box 9.2 (below), Nigel Biggs describes what he and other employers of his acquaintance thought of doctoral level skills, prior to employing PGRs himself.

Why is it that the doctorate is so misunderstood? The answer is simple: only 1% of the population holds a doctoral degree, and we tend not to talk about what it entails all that much. Often we assume people should know. But why should they?

REFLECTION POINT

Think about what you knew about what a doctorate entails before you actually began doctoral studies – there were probably several aspects that came as a surprise as your studies progressed.

People make assumptions based on past experience. Because most employers have an undergraduate degree or at least have a lot of experience with people with such degrees, they understand what a degree is and assume a doctorate is just more of the same, but a bit harder and in more depth. This difference in understanding is evident in employment practices.

It is generally accepted that an undergraduate degree produces people with 'graduate skills'. These are a collection of transferable skills, regardless of undergraduate discipline, which employers recognise as being a valuable asset in many cases. There is as yet little equivalent assumption made for people with a doctorate. Employers assume a person with a doctorate knows more about a given field, but do not always recognise the additional or extended transferable skills such study also confers. People do not understand the doctorate, perhaps, because those with the degree have not communicated its value to the general population sufficiently. This is the problem that underlies the common mistakes researchers make when marketing themselves to non-academic audiences. See an employer's viewpoint in Box 9.2 below.

BOX 9.2 AN EMPLOYER'S PERSPECTIVE ON HIRING PHDS

I only employed a couple of PhDs in my time but they were different from new graduates. The CV outline is the same, but the ones I employed were careful to explain the extra (and very useful) skills they brought to the company – and not just the technical understanding of their PhD topic. Their ability to analyse a topic from all angles was a revelation to me – someone (like many employers) who had thought PhDs were very narrow. The topic may be narrow, but the thinking and analysis is wide and effective.

I did worry that the first researcher I hired would not understand the dynamics of a small business (when we have limited time and funds to research anything). And his work did drag on a bit when he insisted on 'researching' yet more aspects before delivering a conclusion and outline design. But in practice this is no different from software developers always wanting to add another great 'bell' or 'whistle' before releasing the next version. In the end, I just insisted it had to finish 'this week'!

The second researcher was a great developer and the basic source of all our new IP. He loved to expand new ideas and was not bad at customer contact. It was invaluable that he spoke both 'techy' and 'customer' languages, something many PhDs can/should stress in their CV.

These days I also see a niche for PhDs to be good project managers – for those who can speak those two types of language. If a PhD could show that ability I would employ them very quickly!

Nigel Biggs, Entrepreneur-in-Residence, University of Surrey

Mistake #4: Thinking that the doctorate alone will get you the job

Although in the distant past doctorates were so rare that people with them were much sought after, it is important nowadays not to expect that your doctorate is a golden ticket to a job. Just because others applying do not necessarily have a doctorate does not mean you will automatically be given preference. For instance, if a job does not require a doctorate, you are most likely going to be put in the same category as all other graduates, but might be considered too expensive to hire for 'merely a little extra in-depth knowledge' (a misunderstanding mentioned above) or too intellectual/not practical enough, as alluded to above. Therefore, it is up to you to communicate the wide range of professional skills you have gained from your degree and from any research experience afterwards. If you have worked through Chapters 4–7, you will recognise now, if not before, all the other skills your doctorate has helped you develop. Make sure you communicate these skills to potential employers. Make no assumptions that they will know the added value of gaining a doctorate.

Mistake #5: Not communicating what you can do for them

While writing covering letters, and being interviewed, it is natural that you will have a very personal focus on why you would benefit from the job. In contrast, what potential employers want to know are the benefits that you would provide to them: what skills you have that they really need. Transferable skills are highly valued within and outside academia. All you have to do is read a few job adverts to really understand this. Convince yourself of this by working through Activity 9.3.

ACTIVITY 9.3   UNDERSTANDING EMPLOYERS' GENERAL REQUIREMENTS

Search on the website www://jobs.co.uk for jobs outside academia. Find at least three different jobs that interest you at least a little, even if not perfect for you. Read the advertisement, job description and person specification, underlining all the skills and attributes they ask for in their candidates. Do you see any patterns? Are there any skills that all of them want? Are there any differences between jobs about specific skill/attribute requirements? How do they match with what you think you could offer?

It would be worthwhile making a list of those attributes/skills that are commonly required to ensure that you emphasise in future applications that you have them. In contrast, note that each employer has some specific requirements.

If you want to get a job, it is very important that you are able to demonstrate those skills that particular employers value the most. Each CV you submit will have to be tailored to each position, so ensure that you avoid the trap of thinking that one good CV will suffice for every job application. You have to think about what the employer is looking for and bring that out in your covering letter and CV, highlighting for them what you have to offer. In your covering letter, specifically point out how the skills you have developed will benefit them; this letter should act as a bridge between the job on offer and your attributes.

Mistake #6: Over-emphasising the technical above the personal attributes

Focusing on the technical skills you have acquired is natural for someone who has been doing research in a particular field for several years. In addition to being careful to adjust your technical vocabulary so as not to alienate your audience, think also about what else, besides technical expertise, is required to do the job. You may have to fit into a team or even lead a team; you may need to interact with customers as well as fellow workers; you may have to adapt to different working conditions, environmental or cultural. Many non-academic employers care much more about your skills in adapting and fitting in than your technical knowledge.

Showing your skills on your CV and in interviews

Throughout this chapter we have discussed important concepts for effectively marketing yourself, all of which are relevant when putting together your CV. Most of us find it fairly easy to list our achievements on our CV. However, knowing how to communicate your skills effectively, yet concisely, is a challenge. What can be helpful is to create a super CV or a portfolio (see Chapter 8) that contains all of your experience, training and skills, and then think about how you can customise it for each individual application. In your super CV, think about how your experiences are linked to your skills. Note down during which of your experiences (jobs, education, etc.) you particularly developed or demonstrated individual transferable skills (in a similar way to your list of evidence in Activity 8.3). Once you have this complete document, you can look at the job advertisement and tailor your CV for any specific job and prepare yourself for interview by reminding yourself of examples of how and when you demonstrated particular key skills and attributes. Box 9.3 provides tips on putting together a successful CV.

BOX 9.3   TOP TEN CV TIPS

1. **Get advice from an expert**. If you are at a university, there will usually be a careers advisor you can see. If you are not, it is possible that your Alma Mater may offer this service to previous graduates. Take advantage! Failing this, you can use the National Careers Service or a private careers consultant (Association of Career Professionals). It may also be helpful to get a person from the relevant field/profession to have a look at your CV and give you feedback, if possible. This again is where having a strong, broad network may be useful.

2. **Tailor your CV for each job**. Look at the job description and advertisement and make sure you include what they want … and leave out what they do not. Do not underestimate the importance of the 'softer' employability skills. You have to offer the full package – qualifications, experience and employability skills (see Appendix 4).

3. **Do your research**. Beyond the job description, look at the company's or university's website. What is important to them? How are you a good match? Highlight this in your covering letter and CV.

4. **Put the most important information first**. The front page is what they will see first. If it does not grab their attention, they will not look any further. Most employers give every CV a 7/10 second scan first – will your CV pass this test?

5. **Use the words in the job description**. This is especially important when applying to a big company, as they may use a scanning system that throws out applications that do not include the actual words they have used. An electronic scanner will not realise that collaboration and interdisciplinary working could represent the same skill.

6. **Use strong, positive words**. Your language matters, communicate clearly and effectively, using, for example, 'and' instead of 'but'!

7. **Appearance matters**. Use a clear consistent layout which makes it easy to find the relevant information; headings and bullet points can help. Think carefully about the font you use – Times Roman is nowadays old-fashioned and there are considerations to be given for people with reading difficulties so use a font such as Arial to make the task easier for all.

8. **Make it concise**. In general, for the non-academic CV you should only have two pages. For the academic CV you can use more, but there is still no room for falsely padding it out. Some font types take less room, such as Arial Narrow. Try to avoid using a very small font size – if it is difficult to read, it will not be read!

9. **Proofread well**. Spelling and grammar mistakes do not leave a good impression. Remember that spellcheck facilities alone are inadequate – they do not differentiate 'their' from 'there', for instance.

(Continued)

(Continued)

10. **A good covering letter matters**. A covering letter is a connecting document, connecting the CV to the job and organisation. The covering letter is primarily about the organisation and the job you are applying for. Your CV is about you – the covering letter is about them. What is interesting about this career, organisation and job to you must be followed by a concise description of why YOU are the best candidate for THEM, highlighting how you meet any specific requirements they may have. Remember that what interests them is what you can do to contribute to the success of the department/organisation – not what they will do for you.

Ann Henderson, Careers Adviser for Researchers, University of Surrey

There are some specific differences between the academic and non-academic CV that are helpful to consider when preparing your CV for a specific job. The first is that, although two pages is generally the absolute maximum length for a non-academic CV, an academic CV generally includes lists of presentations and publications which demonstrate the academic credibility of your work. Non-academic employers might maximally be interested in the number rather than the detail of such activities. However, hobbies and personal statements are not common on the academic CV, whereas they can be highly valued by employers from other sectors seeking indicators of personal attributes. In Box 9.4 a business employer describes what he looks for in the CV.

BOX 9.4   A NON-ACADEMIC EMPLOYER'S PERSPECTIVE ON CVS

I would look for a quick summary at the top of the CV (or possibly elsewhere on page 1 but certainly no further) and use that to guide my interest to look further down – or reject it. Ten-second scan at most.

For me, the best 'summaries' are a list of keywords about the person and not a 'personal statement'. Most of those all sound the same. Everyone says the same thing one way or another. I like to see things like engineer, designer, technical author, software geek, hardware hobbyist, passionate about playing the flute, degree at evening classes, etc. In a few words, I get a sense of the whole person, including a key hobby or two. This gives an indication of whether the person will fit into our culture, our teams.

That is what makes a particular CV different enough to look at again.

> The next scan means a complete read through, probably when I will see the qualifications and experiences – and, importantly, any comments about their relevance to the job applied for. A covering letter that shows interest in (and some knowledge of) the job helps immensely too.
>
> Nigel Biggs, Entrepreneur-in-Residence, University of Surrey

In this chapter, we have explored various ways in which you can more effectively market your skills and experience to enhance your employability (also see Appendix 4, the Employability Skills Questionnaire). The key is to understand what your potential employers care about and to clearly articulate how you can deliver it. The ways to become an expert at this is to get out there and talk to as many different people as possible. This will not only help you develop your communication skills, but will also allow you to establish a broader network of contacts and an understanding of a wider range of perspectives. Although most of these new contacts will not be your future employers, they may well be collaborators, referees, informants or friends who will help and support you throughout your career.

Ideas for further reading

Becker, L. And Denicolo, P. (2012) *Success in Research: Publishing Journal Articles.* London: Sage.

Denicolo, P. and Becker, L. (2012) *Success in Research: Developing Research Projects.* London: Sage.

Wilson, H. (2007) *The Little Black Book of Career Success.* Manchester: Cheeky Monkey Publishing.

National Careers Service at: https://nationalcareersservice.direct.gov.uk/advice/getajob/cvs/Pages/default.aspx.

Prospects: The official graduate careers website at: www.prospects.ac.uk/.

Vitae has a range of 'What Do Researchers Do?' resources and reports, including:

What Do Researchers Do? Early Career Progression of Doctoral Graduates (2013) available at: www.vitae.ac.uk/policy-practice/513201/What-do-researchers-do.html.

Search the internet for 'how to write a CV'.

10

HOW CAN RESEARCHERS MAKE A SUCCESSFUL TRANSITION TO ANOTHER EMPLOYMENT?

Chapter overview

This chapter discusses:

- Some of the peculiarities of the research/academic environment that distinguish it from other working environments
- Key areas of 'cultural' difference, including:
  - Office etiquette and administrative skills
  - Communication
  - Business acumen and strategic thinking
  - Team working and relationship building

We will consider how knowledge of these areas of difference can help you to successfully navigate between work cultures.

The peculiarities of Higher Education

A question that may arise with increasing vigour towards the end of your current project might be: How do you make a successful transition from the academic research environment to other kinds of work, even if it is still within a university?

Although the skills and even some of the knowledge required of the academic and non-academic sectors may be the same or very similar (especially knowledge of the transferable kind – see Box 10.1 below), the behaviours and expected modes of working are not. The cultures can be very different, and no matter how long or short your experience of working within an academic environment has been, you will have adapted to that culture and learnt to operate in that environment. Further, you may not yet recognise how acculturated (or institutionalised) you have become.

Much of what you have learned will have been unconscious acquisition so you will need to develop a heightened self-awareness about your attributes, especially if you later find yourself working in a situation where the people do things very differently from the way you have been used to. While it would be necessary, in any case, to understand the culture or ways of doing things when making any move, even to a new department within the same institution, in making a successful transition from academia to another kind of employment researchers must become aware of some key differences as these kinds of moves will require greater levels of change and adaptation.

Work in Higher Education (HE) is distinctive, particularly in the way it is organised, carried out and disseminated. Adjusting to a different tempo of work, along with the differing values and conventions of a new workplace, may present a challenge in unexpected ways. For instance, independent action and ways of working, common in academia, may be mediated in other sectors by management and reporting mechanisms, while the way work is organised and communicated will be very different from what will, undoubtedly, have become an established form of working for the average researcher. A frequently noted area of difference is in the meeting of deadlines; in other working environments deadlines can be much deadlier or, as one ECR on a placement remarked, 'they are drop-dead deadlines'. Unlike academia, there may be little or no negotiable margin of manoeuvrability and failure to meet requirements will carry consequences, not just for you, but also elsewhere in the organisation. In addition, the need for transparency and accountability in other sectors can be more intense, while the ability to be a 'good colleague' and participate fully in a team will be an essential requirement.

Nevertheless, be assured that the good habits and qualities that make outstanding researchers are those needed in non-academic roles, albeit modified to fit the context. Although you may need to make some adjustment to your working practices and behaviours, the skills you need to be a successful academic are the same skills/attributes required of any successful manager or leader in the corporate or public sector. Box 10.1 summarises the key areas.

> **BOX 10.1   SKILLS/ATTRIBUTES REQUIRED OF ACADEMICS AND ANY MANAGER OR LEADER IN OTHER SECTORS**
>
> Excellent project, time and people management skills, 'emotional intelligence' and business awareness
>
> Team working, networking and leadership skills
>
> An understanding of the broader sector and context
>
> Negotiation, influence and persuasion skills
>
> Communication skills, both written and oral
>
> Creative thinking, problem-solving, analytical skills
>
> Self-confidence, risk-taking and risk management skills
>
> Budget management, numerical and IT skills
>
> Strategic thinking skills and financial acumen
>
> Enthusiasm and integrity
>
> And, finally, specialist knowledge of some kind.

Michael Eraut has explored the movement between what he describes as the 'knowledge cultures of higher education' and those of other kinds of workplace environments. He noted that:

> performance in the workplace typically involves the integration of several different forms of knowledge and skill, under conditions that allow little time for the analytic/deliberative approach favoured in higher education. (Eraut 2009: 65)

Failure to appreciate the extent to which context influences learning can result in a serious misjudgement of how difficult it is to cross boundaries. Much of the knowledge you will encounter in the workplace is taken for granted (as it is in HE) and requires experience of the situation to understand it. This can present the researcher fresh out of academe with a real challenge, especially as the personal knowledge and prior experience you have learned in the HE context or culture will be clearly visible in your present performance and workplace behaviour. So while we applaud the focus on transferable skills, we nevertheless recognise, with Eraut, the magnitude of the 'transferring' task. It is not a straightforward mapping, so perhaps we should re-name them 'translatable skills'!

Every employer wants someone who can settle into a new role and team quickly; yet the chances may be quite high that you do not possess the same level of skill as an employee who has been working in the environment for the same amount of time that you have been in research – and the longer you have been in HE the more likely this is. Some of the differences will be in very basic skills peculiar to the context, including the four key work areas discussed below. An obvious danger is that both your employer and you as an employee will over-estimate your knowledge and capability in the new environment. It may be assumed that because you have a doctorate you must be highly capable – and indeed you are, but perhaps not immediately so in all the respects expected in a new role. If you have been actively involved in extra-mural activities during your career as a researcher, you may find you are better fitted for the working environment than the average graduate, but you may still have a lot to learn. Fortunately, as we saw in Chapter 9, researchers have a range of attributes that employers are extremely interested in.

Employers will value the independent thinking that researchers offer but not, we hasten to add, too much independent action! They will love your ability to distil and synthesise information very quickly, your capacity to 'think outside the box', the mental risk-taking and problem-solving. You will be able to analyse a situation quickly, cut to the heart of a problem and see the broader context, and you will do this more quickly, with greater depth and sophistication than a good first degree graduate. Employers will appreciate your academic rigour (to a point, as noted in the employer's first example in Box 9.2) but you need to make sure that it aligns with business processes; and they will applaud your potential to grow the job – but you need to be able *to do* the job before you can begin to grow it or develop it any way.

Adapting to a new environment should be straightforward if you approach it as you would any research topic; that is, you will need to assess the environment to confirm what are the operational and etiquette codes. Just as you would if you moved between disciplines or worked collaboratively with another research area, you need to define your terms and audit the style of the context in which you are operating to confirm that you are all speaking the same language, have the same understandings of success and can agree what good performance looks like.

Office etiquette and administrative skills

It is arguable that an organisation will only be as good as its basic office and administrative processes, which include: consistent and coherent procedures, good customer service, good record keeping, clear paper/audit trails, and the use of IT. Office etiquette and good administrative skills are frequently taken for granted and often undervalued, but they are the foundation stones of every successful organisation. They are seen as so basic that everyone must be able to do them. However, keeping clear and easily accessible records either in filing cabinets or online is an art form. You might consider whether your files and folders are readily useable by others, are in a logical order and easy to find. In the UK Civil Service they have (or had) a manual on how to file in alphabetical order, which seems ridiculous until you realise that any member of staff should be able to move from one department to another anywhere in the country and know precisely where to find a paper for a 'Dr MacDonald', whether it is spelt with as *Mac* or a *Mc*. Unless you know what the basic structure and systems are for the organisation's processes and functions, you may find you are wasting a lot of time and energy or, worse, upsetting your colleagues and confirming suspicions that PGRs and ECRs have their 'heads in the clouds'.

How does this translate into practice?

- Work must be well organised and easily accessed by others; there should always be a paper or audit trail: a clear record of who did what, when and why. If, for some reason, you cannot make it into the workplace, that task you were working must not come to a halt because the organisation and team still have to function.
- The 'customer' (who may be your internal colleagues and not just a 'sales' customer) is always right: well, they may not be, but it is wise not to get into an argument with them. Seek to resolve problems, not to blame others. Quickly address the issue, perhaps with advice from your line manager or colleague, and move on.

We all use email but you cannot assume that you use it in the way your new employer expects you to use it. Modes of address and greetings may be too informal for the environment, especially if your status has changed. Be smart and take your cue from others. Ask for sample emails or ask your line manager if they could approve your emails for a few weeks until you get settled. It can be especially challenging to understand the etiquette of writing emails in the English language if it is not your native form of communication. However, it would be useful for anyone new to an organisation to ask to be copied into emails for a few months, so that you can learn to imitate the language style used in that context. Indeed, it is a good idea to find an exemplar, someone well respected in your new environment, whose behaviour is a good role model and whom you can emulate. Better still, get them to mentor you! Of course, you would not be adopting a new attribute in doing this; you have already had a similar experience in adapting to a strange world, and have survived it successfully, in your early years of becoming a researcher.

Communication

Communication outside academia differs considerably in both frequency and kind. You cannot underestimate the need to communicate with colleagues in both detail and extent, and this is not an affront to your ability to do the job; it is simply the way it is. Communication is likely to be more regular and inclusive than you have been used to. For example, you may have to provide daily updates to your line manager or go into a 'huddle' for informal briefings. On the whole, academics are not required to give a regular account of themselves or to keep people informed on a daily/weekly basis; largely they are expected to get on with their work.

As a doctoral researcher you may have had monthly or weekly supervisions. As a postdoc you may have had monthly meetings with your PI and they may have been very informal. Most academics and researchers are required to submit an end-of-year report but this is usually for the funders rather than for line management or performance purposes, while appraisal systems vary wildly throughout the sector, especially for postdocs on fixed-term contracts and who may seldom experience a formal appraisal. Other than that, reporting mechanisms are fairly informal. Even national assessments of research occur several years apart, as, for example, with the Research Excellence Framework (REF) in the UK. All of this is in complete contrast to non-academic employment where it seems you can never communicate enough.

You may find the increased intensity of communication a challenge to what you perceive as your 'power, authority, or position'. However, proving yourself to be trusted takes time; without this, problems will undoubtedly occur. More importantly, line managers need to have a clear picture of what is going on, not because they are trying to do your job for you but because they will be required to explain, promote or defend the team's activities to a whole range of people, including their senior management team and other departments. It may be useful to think of this, as well as approach it, as super-reporting to a funder.

University employees often encounter problems that might be assumed (rightly or wrongly) to be handled more effectively in a non-university environment. While collegially this has lots of advantages, it also contains limitations. For example, it is not uncommon to find university staff, untrained in people management, thrust into managing difficult fellow academics. The results can be avoidance or confrontation rather than constructive problem-solving. Few people find this aspect of communication easy (see Chapter 7) but other employers might expect a greater degree of confidence in such situations.

On the positive side, academics are very good at communicating their research and ideas to others so, in this respect, you will probably excel in the workplace. However, presenting information is only one aspect of communication skills. The style in which academics present their work, and which usually pervades the bulk of their communication, can sometimes seem to be didactic, directive or talking 'at' people. Although the ability to formulate ideas and to present and defend them publically is an important skill, it is also important to remember that this is not the only form of communication. A skilled teacher, for example, will be able to engage with their students to tease out what they think. So be aware that other kinds of work may involve other forms of communication and it will be important to ensure any message or instruction has been understood as was intended. If you are unsure you have been understood or have understood correctly, ask for confirmation or for feedback from those you are communicating with.

A common people management approach in non-academic environments is to use a coaching style. Initially, researchers may find coaching styles difficult; it is contrary to how they have learned to behave and treat people because, as with skilled teaching above, the essence of coaching is to be 'non-directive'. It may be a good idea to be life-coached yourself so you can experience what it is like and then acquire some coaching skills so you can appreciate the style and how to adopt it. Being non-directive can be a challenge, especially if you are used to having to give instruction. The notion of 'equality of thought' (the basis of many coaching approaches) can be testing, as can including everyone in a discussion and respecting ideas that may seem stupid or inappropriate, especially for those who find it difficult to resist leaping in with expert knowledge to correct colleagues. However, managers spend a lot of time coaching staff (that is, actively encouraging improved performance) and enabling staff (all of them) to come to their own solutions. While universities might benefit enormously from coaching, most departments in them have a long way to go to before they realise the potential of coaching. Among other professions, though, engaging in the coaching process is seen as *the* mechanism for making progress in your career. Activity 10.1 may help you on the path to an effective coaching style.

ACTIVITY 10.1 IDENTIFYING WHETHER YOU USE A COACHING STYLE OF COMMUNICATION

In discussing an important topic, do you regularly tell people, for instance, friends, family and colleagues, what you think without asking what they think first? YES/NO

Do you give people advice even if they have not asked for it? YES/NO

Do you find yourself saying: 'have you tried …' YES/NO

Or 'if I were you, I'd do/try/think …' YES/NO

If you said yes to any of the above, you should practise active listening, which includes: being attentive with your whole body not just your ears; avoiding distracting thoughts or thinking about how you might respond (await your turn); seeking clarity rather than assuming you have understood the speaker's intentions; encouraging the speaker with your positive body language. Next time you find yourself about to offer advice, substitute it with 'What do you think should be done?'

Try to get into the habit of listening to others instead of coming up with all the answers all of the time. Everyone will know you are intelligent, so help create the space for others to shine and build their confidence. This aspect of work begins to move you into a people management or leadership role, whereby it is not about you but about getting the best from those around you.

Business acumen and strategic thinking

It is a regular complaint of employers that graduates, postgraduates and academic staff lack business sense so there has been much effort by universities to understand the needs of employers. However, in all fairness to HEIs, the main purpose of research is not, necessarily, to acquire business skills, unless, of course, you happen to be in a business and management school or have a research product obviously ripe for business exploitation. We agree, however, that some business skills are equally advantageous in the academic environment and certainly an understanding of your chosen 'business' (education) is essential if you wish to pursue a career within it. For example, the ability to spot developing trends in research funding and topics, both nationally and internationally, would be expedient in career-building terms. Activity 10.2 will help identify your current business acumen.

ACTIVITY 10.2   WHERE DOES THE MONEY COME FROM?

Some of the most important questions involve money. Crudely put, where is it, how much is there and who has control of it? Perhaps the most significant question of all is about how (or even whether) you can influence the spending of it.

(Continued)

(Continued)

Do you know how the finances for your department work? For example, where does the money come from and how much is there? What is it spent on and who decides how it is spent?

Similarly, do you know how individual grants operate?

What is the turnover, to the nearest £10,000 equivalent, of your institution?

Do you know how your institution and department are financed? How much comes from teaching, research, public and private funding, donations and business commissions?

How does the impact of research affect the income of your institution?

Understanding finances – the funding of projects and organisations – is one aspect of business acumen. It also involves leadership qualities and entails being able to make judgements and decisions that affect the business (hopefully) in a good way. This may mean applying your research skills in their more analytical than applied mode. If you get into the habit of understanding the broader context and taking an interest in the organisation you are working for, this will be a useful skill applicable to all kinds of work environments. So, for example, you should be able to scan the horizon to see whether your research is in a growth area or can be linked into a growth area (where there is likely to be future funding) or whether you are in an area in which it may be difficult to attract funding. Do you know what the strategic ambitions are of the research council or main funding body for your area? If not, how can you find out? Do you also know the aims of the other research councils/funders and can you pick out any trends in the sector? Usually, an idea in one area will make its way to the others eventually, the development of collaborative centres of research excellence being an example. Do you have an understanding of the national HE picture and trends? Do you get regular news feeds on your computer or mobile, and are they related to your area of work or just general news? Do you know what international developments are taking place in your area of research or the work you aspire to do? Even difficult questions need to be considered, such as: where are the growth markets in HE and will your discipline exist in its current form in a decade's time?

The key is to develop a more sophisticated understanding of what you do and how it is positioned in the 'business area' you are working within and to continue to maintain a current interest in the wider developments affecting your field rather than focusing only on particular aspects within it. You can then translate the business skills and methods you have acquired into the areas of work you aspire to.

REFLECTION POINT

Consider the questions we have raised in this section and how you might develop your knowledge in this area.

Team working and relationship building

Are you a good colleague and what does that mean? Team working, or rather the perceived lack of it, is another area employers are often concerned about when employing someone from academia. In STEMM subjects, you may have belonged to a team that was hierarchical (even if it appeared 'flat') so your experience may be of working in a team but not of the team working that employers' value. Those from HASS disciplines are less likely to have team-work experience so may have more to learn. In either case, you will need to have a clear understanding of your role within the team so that you are able to make a full and positive contribution, which enhances your own performance as well as that of your colleagues. Establishing, building and maintaining good working relationships can be a challenge, especially if you have been used to working alone or on your own project for some time.

Successful teams need a diverse population and good mix of 'talents' to thrive, so it is worth spending some time considering how you establish new relationships and, once you have made them, how to build and maintain them. Although we all much prefer working with people we like, it is not a necessary requirement and in some cases may not even be possible. As professionals, we are required to be able to work with all kinds of people and find ways of making our relationships function in a productive manner. This relies on the principles of mutual respect, accepting equality of thought and being open, honest and transparent in our interactions and transactions with each other – issues we discussed in Chapter 7. As in research, a key person with whom you need to make a good relationship is your line manager. Again, your research skills will be useful in discovering their management style. A helpful attitude can be that your role is to make your line manager's life as easy as possible, which does not imply being servile. Rather, it means anticipating what they need from you that would assist them to do their job better. Please note that you will need to deliver 'the goods' rather than simply the offer of help.

Transparency and being able to discuss work issues openly are central to a good working relationship, so there cannot be any surprises for your line manager or anyone else in the organisation. Indeed, the professional relationship you have with your doctoral supervisor or PI should work in the same way. Good colleagues everywhere share information, work in an open, collaborative and communal way, are committed to the team's objectives and keep everyone concerned with a project well informed and up to date. If you have come from an environment where there were suspicions that junior researchers did not receive full recognition for their contribution, then you may find the concept of open sharing difficult, but be alert to its importance in a different environment. Eventually you will need to trust your colleagues.

If you do not share your ideas and report your activities, at best, your line manager will not be able to give you credit for the work you have done and the contribution you have made, while, at worst, they will not be able to defend you should criticisms be made of your work and the way you have gone about things. Co-workers need to know what you are doing, planning and thinking *before* you do it, rather than afterwards, just as your research supervisor/PI would want to be included, informed and kept up to date, though perhaps not as regularly as a non-academic manager may need.

In HE, researchers are valued for being autonomous and independent learners. Indeed, this is one of the major achievements of a doctorate (along with the completing the thesis itself). Yet in other kinds of working environments independent working, even if conducted with the best of intentions, such as not wishing to be a pest to anyone by asking lots of questions, can be seen as secretive and unteam-like behaviour. Where line managers do express concern over a lack of team working, this will be about something more fundamental than your ability to 'get stuck in' or 'get the job done'. It will be about putting the team and/or the organisation *before* your own interests.

It is an accepted academic behaviour to believe all views are equally valid (although of course some are obviously more valid than others), so you may disagree intellectually with your academic colleagues, arguing your point with evidence to substantiate it. However, this is not necessarily a useful attitude to maintain in other situations where your line manager may not be expressing a 'view' or 'opinion', but their professional judgement and requirements. You may be able to question that judgement if you can put across a valid business case, but remember that, unlike in your research topic, you may not be in full possession of the facts or understand the context in which decisions are being made, so your views may be rejected. Line managers will not expect to debate every issue, although, of course, if there are important or major differences of view, you need to discuss this openly and constructively with your line manager. In this way you can avoid a problematic working relationship and potentially looking for another job!

One of the greatest areas of difficulty in transitioning to a new role may be psychological, that is, finding or establishing a sense of place and building relationships accordingly. Dealing with a change of environment is never easy. The reality may be that your doctorate or research work may initially appear not to count for much in your new job, whether within or outside academia. You may find that you are not the person on the team with the most professional skill, knowledge or experience. Certainly, as we have noted, you will have considerable professional skills to offer, but you need to find out which ones are most needed for the role and what you need to acquire or improve as necessary. Fortunately, you can use the skills you do have as a researcher to figure it all out very quickly, probably within 3–6 months.

If you do not take the opportunity to investigate which skills are needed in a new role, you may be in danger of assuming you know what skills are required and act accordingly. This could lead to a superficial performance in your new job or a form of behaviour that is otherwise known as 'playing at the job', whereby you do all the things you think the job is about rather than those that are actually required. This could result, for example, in overly confident behaviour (such as making inappropriate decisions, taking responsibility above your level of knowledge, experience and/or competence) or in the inappropriate delegation of tasks to junior (or even senior) colleagues. In all work contexts, people appreciate newcomers who are willing to learn and adapt.

REFLECTION POINT

How would or do you feel about taking a role outside academia? Are you keen to take on the challenge of a new environment, desperate to leave the academic one, or apprehensive about the change? Are you proud of your academic achievements or do you hide them from non-academics? Any one of these feelings will require working through. You need to understand your own motivations and reservations if you are to project a positive impression to others. If you are not comfortable with yourself, the chances are you will not meet your new colleagues and working situation on equal and accepting terms, making any adaption to work all the more difficult for you and them.

It is difficult, when you have climbed to the top of a mountain peak and barely had time to savour the sense of achievement, to then find that you have to master a new set of foothills before climbing to the next peak. However, dealing with this sense of 'starting all over again' is a skill in itself that permeates the life of a researcher in that every new project is another mountain in the range or another sea in which to swim. When you find your own way of meeting each new challenge and know you have acquired the skills that enable you to confidently 'start over' or move forward, then you have moved into the realms of the final transferable skill, which takes us to the last chapter of this book.

Ideas for further reading

Search the internet for 'How to be a good employee'.

Brinkman, R. and Kirschner, R. (2002) *Dealing with People You Can't Stand: How to Bring Out the Best in People at Their Worst*. New York: McGraw-Hill.

Find out who the ten most unwanted team characters are!

Eraut, M. (2009) 'The transfer of knowledge between education and workplace settings', in H. Daniels, H. Lauder and J. Porter (eds), *Knowledge, Values and Educational Policy: A Critical Perspective*. Abingdon, UK: Routledge.

Kline, N. (1999) *Time to Think: Listening to Ignite the Human Mind*. London: Ward Lock, Cassell Illustrated.

Researchers may enjoy Kline's concept of the 'thinking environment' to enable great thought.

Whitmore, J. (2009) *Coaching for Performance: GROWing Human Potential and Purpose – the Principles and Practice of Coaching and Leadership* (4th edition). People Skills for Professionals Series. London: Nicholas Brealey.

There are some great tips on active listening available on the web, for example: www.mindtools. com/CommSkll/ActiveListening.htm (retrieved 10/2012). www.ccl.org/leadership/ podcast/transcriptTheBig6.aspx (retrieved 10/2012).

11

HOW CAN TRANSFERABLE SKILLS BECOME AN INTEGRAL PART OF LIFE?

Chapter overview

This chapter discusses:

- Career management
- Specific cohorts
- Expanding your CV
- Continuing professional development (CPD)

Introduction

Being a researcher at any stage, from early in a doctoral programme to being an ECR looking for the next post, you have the unique privilege of studying a subject you enjoy, surrounded by the most extraordinary mix of talented people, and in environments with unparalleled access to opportunities and ideas. Higher Education (HE) affords researchers at every stage and from all backgrounds a range of prospects that does not exist in other working environments, yet may require effort to realise. We know that being a researcher can be challenging, occasionally boring, and it may present you with uncertainties about your future. Should you feel demotivated, consider the broader picture and congratulate yourself on how much you have achieved. Setting yourself small goals, and congratulating yourself on achieving them, is not only motivating in tough times but also a useful habit to get into for managing your career and helping you move on.

This is our final point about transferable skills – acquiring and improving them should become routine.

Managing your career

For those who do not have a clear career plan, or indeed life plan, the usual career management advice focuses on working out a number of key attributes and desires, and then using these as the basis for further exploration into career possibilities. Although jobs for life are a rarity these days, the usual approach invites you to consider: what kind of person you are, or who you would like to become; what you like and dislike; what kind of organisation you might like to work for; what motivates you and is important to you; what you value; what your strengths and weaknesses are, and so on. When you put all of the pieces together, it usually generates a sense of direction that can be both clear and diffuse. For example, you may firmly conclude that you love science, enjoy writing and explaining ideas to different audiences but that you are not willing to travel far because of family commitments, although you may be happy to leave academia. None of this indicates a specific role but, when combined, could direct you to a range of opportunities. Potential jobs might include: a writer for a publisher of medical or scientific material for trade and industry; a liaison role in industry to help with collaborative projects with universities; a project management or design role in any kind of business; teaching roles in the primary or tertiary sectors; a consultant in your own business. You may be a HASS researcher and love research but have been unable to secure a postdoctoral position, so you could explore the options for conducting research in or for a range of government bodies, national and international organisations, industry, charities, or go freelance. The possibilities are endless but they all come down to what suits you and what you would really like to do.

Professionals find being coached by a professional careers coach very helpful for gaining clarity in this process. The idea is that if you are largely (say 80% of your time) working to your strengths and interests, values and motivations, you will be fulfilled in your role. The problem with academia is that, although it can provide a powerful and enriching research experience, research and academic posts are limited. Nevertheless, we urge you to consider that 'the world is your oyster' in terms of your career prospects; indeed, the whole purpose of this book has been to enable you to realise the potential you have worked hard to acquire by virtue of being a researcher!

Reprinted with kind permission of Dr Tania-Morgan Alcantarilla, University of Southampton. March 2013

My career goal for the **next** year:	6 months review date:	Did I achieve my goal? Yes ☐ No ☐
	End of year review date:	Did I achieve my goal? Yes ☐ No ☐
I will grow my CV this year by doing something new in the area of:		
My career goal for the next 2 years:	6 months review dates:	Did I achieve my goal? Yes ☐ No ☐
	Final review date:	Did I achieve my goal? Yes ☐ No ☐
I will grow my CV next year by doing something new in the area of:		
Action Plan		

Actions that will help me achieve my career goal	Training that will help me to achieve my career goal	Experience that will help me achieve my career goal (including any volunteering or networking activity)	Obstacles I need to overcome to achieve my career goal	Actions to overcome these obstacles	Support I need to achieve my career goal

FIGURE 11.1 Career plan template

Managing your career, however, will require attention and hard work and should not be left to the last minute: you should be working on it all of the time rather than confirming the old careers services' adage that 'most people spend more time planning their holidays than they do planning their careers'. Although the orthodox career management view is that you should be planning two to three years ahead, since time spent as a PGR and ECR is quite short, we advocate planning on an annual basis as well as for the longer term. You may find Figure 11.1, the career plan template, useful for beginning to plan your career direction.

Careers are built over decades, requiring some planning to ensure at least that the next position flows upwards (or sometimes sideways) from the previous one. Success depends on knowing where you want to go and figuring out what you need to get there, continuously building on your previous experience and knowledge, learning new things, improving and expanding your skill set. This process involves forward thinking and backward reviewing, which is why a professional development plan (PDP) (discussed in Chapter 8) is useful. Role models and mentors, discussed below, are a great source of inspiration and advice in this respect.

You need to start determining now which role you will be applying for when your contract or project comes to an end. Looking at job descriptions is a useful way of identifying which skills you need so you can take opportunities to fill any gaps while you are still in the stimulating and rich learning environment of your university (see 'Building your CV', below). Be creative in seeking opportunities to gain and enhance your skill set as well as exploring the options and likely career paths in your own and other institutions/organisations. You might begin by exploring the real local career prospects following Activity 11.1 and then expand your horizons.

ACTIVITY 11.1 WHAT IS THE TYPICAL CAREER PATHWAY IN YOUR INSTITUTION?

Can you find out what the staff profile is for your institution? How many temporary contracts are converted to permanent roles? What is the ratio of research to teaching only and mixed portfolio staff, and at what level? What is the typical career pathway for a researcher in your university?

Specific cohorts

In general, PGRs early in their research careers should take advantage of introductory workshops and seek advice to identify, consolidate and expand their transferable skill set, whereas ECRs should aim to improve their general skill set and also to acquire and polish some of the more complex professional skills, such as leadership, financial management and strategic thinking. Both PGRs and ECRs should make the most of their time in HE to build a range of professional relationships as well as their CV (see below), while specific cohorts of researchers have differing needs and may find the following advice helpful.

Part-time researchers need a good deal of tenacity and exceptional time management skills to complete their research projects. Indeed, part-timers will be an excellent source of inspiration for any full-time researcher and should be able to offer advice to other researchers on how to manage a full workload and time effectively. It is important for part-timers to set aside regular time (small or large blocks) for research and to plan training into overall research plans. Their flexible and adaptable approach and experience of managing a range of tasks is well suited to a full-time academic role.

Mature researchers and professional doctorate researchers will already possess an extensive skill set, although they may be lacking in some of the research-related skills discussed in Chapter 4. It is as important to remember that training and development is a fast-moving world so these researchers may need simultaneously to monitor two areas of development, in their current profession and in research. These researchers, along with part-time researchers, may find they need to make an extra effort to remain alert to, or in contact with, important developments in their university context.

Women in academia and in STEMM subjects face particular challenges. They will need to be assiduous in creating professional networks and raising their profiles. Thriving in a male-dominated environment requires a pro-active response and support, which can be obtained from groups in institutions such as 'Women in Science, Engineering and Technology' (WiSET) or those linked to 'Athena SWAN' (the Athena SWAN (the Scientific Women's Academic Network) Charter, along with the work of WiSET, aim to increase the participation and representation of women in STEMM subjects).

International researchers, generally speaking, have been among the most enthusiastic supporters of the skills training and development agenda in the UK. Yet, they may need to consider the nature of the work they plan to take up when they return to their home countries and actively work on developing skills germane to that context.

Building your CV

This is an area where you will need to be proactive (see Chapter 8) to take advantage of the exceptional opportunities in universities to experiment with and gain from a range of experiences around you – turning serendipity to your advantage. In doing so, it will be helpful to plan and pace your learning. For example, one year your focus could be on writing and publishing; next it could be on developing your people management or personal effectiveness skills through mentoring students or public engagement. What is essential is that you build your CV and improve on it year on year. Below are some development areas of direct relevance to researchers.

Impact generation

Although all researchers hope that their research will be significant in some way and make a difference, recently the notion of being able to analyse, measure, articulate and defend the impact that your research makes has become a priority. Evidence of research impact includes citations, the quality of the journals that accept your articles, presentations at conferences accepted through peer review or by invitation, reports of the results of your research being integrated into practice, and so on.

Another book in this series, *Success in Research: Achieving Impact*, provides discussions about various kinds of impact and how they might be measured. Academic employers will be especially interested in the value of your previous research in terms of how well it was received, recognised and evaluated by your peer community, and how you will ensure that impact will be built into your future research.

REFLECTION POINT 〰️

Consider how you could indicate the impact that your research has made, is making, or might make. Do you collect evidence such as citations or a list of invitations? Could you provide a short, cogent argument about the potential of your research to make a difference?

Income and funding generation

As we write, there is a global financial crisis so all prospective employers are highly sensitive to financial issues, particularly generating income of some sort to maintain or enhance their activities. In the research world, in particular, there is a need to know where the potential sources of income are and how best to access them. This will be all too familiar to you if you had to source the funds to support your current research. *Success in Research: Developing Research Proposals*, another book in this series, includes several sections and an extensive appendix on identifying and understanding how best to gain access to funding sources. You may also find that your institution provides workshops on this topic and also on how to create income in entrepreneurial ways (see 'Enterprise' below). It is a good idea to be prepared for employer interview questions on the topic and show that you are at least aware of the internal and external funders of research in your field, their main requirements and the critical steps in the process of acquiring funding.

REFLECTION POINT

In your research area, who are the main sources of funding? Can you identify alternative sources of funding for specific aspects of research?

Financial/budget management

There will be few of you who have never had to manage your own personal finances and budget for necessities. Many of you will have had to provide evidence to programme managers or funders that you manage your maintenance grant or stipend adequately. All will have had a restricted amount of money with which to conduct your research project.

The challenge of dealing with those experiences will have contributed to the skills related to developing and implementing a budget for the daily life of research. These skills will come to the fore when preparing to continue your research through applying for funding to support it. The *Developing Research Proposals* book, mentioned above, has a chapter on preparing a credible budget that will be acceptable to a potential funder while being adequate for you to complete the research. We cannot repeat that here, but we can urge you to think about including in your portfolio some evidence that you can prepare a budget and manage it. Also, your supervisor or PI might be willing to show you examples of budgets included in their proposals.

There are few jobs in the public or private sector that do not include some form of financial management, so acquiring knowledge and understanding in this area, such as recognising what are essential outlays and what are potential sources of savings, would be advantageous.

REFLECTION POINT

If you were challenged in an interview to provide an indication of your ability to manage a budget, what example/s from your prior experience could you draw upon to provide an answer?

Engagement with policy making

Even as a relatively new researcher, it is important to find out what the policies are in your department, school and institution that relate to research practice and also about the process of policy making in those situations. You can make it your business to find out what committees and discussion forums exist, how they work, who they report to, and how final decisions are made; this will improve your 'business' acumen. You might then seek out how to contribute to that process. Most universities encourage PGRs/ECRs to become representatives on policy-making or policy-influencing committees at all levels in the system but, far from there being competition for those places, it is usually difficult to fill them. This could be a good opportunity for you to discover how policy impacts on research and, indeed, how research influences policy. This would be a useful addition to your CV and employers will readily recognise the skill of being a contributing member of a policy-making body, even if you are not able to directly influence policy outside your institution.

REFLECTION POINT

How many times have you wondered why things are done in the way they are and, more cogently, why are they not done better? Perhaps taking the opportunity to sit on a committee might answer some of those questions and help you to develop skills of steering others around to your viewpoint.

Teaching

If you have any opportunity to take on a teaching or demonstrating role during your early years as a researcher, we would suggest that you take it with high expectations of what you might learn from engaging with those roles. First, in addition to providing you with a chance to share topics that you are enthusiastic about, you will gain a greater understanding of them when you try to explain them to others. Secondly, teaching those who are newer than you to those topics also serves to reinforce your confidence in giving presentations while obliging you to think about organising your ideas and material in ways to suit different audiences. Further, this situation puts you in touch with others in your field to add to your network of fellow enthusiasts. If you do not have the opportunity to teach, you could volunteer to help an existing lecturer or simply ask if you can sit in and observe some of their classes. Such offers are likely to be warmly received and may open the way to a 'guest lecture' slot based on your research – after all, you are at the cutting-edge of ideas and have something to offer.

REFLECTION POINT 〰️

Thinking about teaching and learning you have experienced, what other benefits might accrue from engaging in teaching that could strengthen your portfolio?

We suggest that taking or making such opportunities at the very least may help you to decide whether, or not, to pursue a teaching career. There is a plethora of books and research articles about teaching in Higher Education, including the series book *Success in Research: Teaching in Higher Education,* which has been especially written for newer researchers who take up these opportunities. The Society for Research in Higher Education (SRHE) has interest groups that meet to discuss topics relevant to this, while many universities provide training courses in teaching which you might be able to join.

Mentoring

Related to teaching is the role of mentor. You may have had experience of being mentored yourself, that is, having someone more experienced to support and advise you in a particular field of activity. This role is usually less formal than a teaching or supervision role, although some organisations have established mentoring schemes you can join. Generally, though, a mentor is someone who helps a junior or new colleague to find their way around, not simply geographically but culturally. They can provide guidance on where to find resources or how to access them, make introductions to key gatekeepers (who has the key to the stationery cupboard is one important one), alert you to common pitfalls as well as traditions of practice. However, mentoring is not just something done to you, but something you can do for others.

There is as much to be learnt from being a mentor as from being the mentee. Sometimes it is only when you try to convey what 'we do around here' that you actually challenge whether it is the most sensible way of doing things. However, to some extent more importantly, you learn and practise the social skills of inducting others into a new working environment so that they appreciate it rather than fear it. You may now recognise that you did something similar with new students, perhaps in a buddy system, which could be included in your CV, or you may spot an opportunity to become a mentor to someone in your work/study environment. Your institution may have some guidelines for its more formal mentoring system that you also could learn from. This can be a win–win situation as the help and guidance you provide is simultaneously developing your skills.

REFLECTION POINT

Have you completed a writing task or similar on time because you intended to share it with a mentor? What tasks could you share with a mentee? How might this contribute to your portfolio?

Public engagement

Sharing knowledge with the public has long been an activity in which researchers have been involved, but recently 'public engagement' or 'knowledge exchange/transfer' has become a growth area that affords a considerable range of opportunity for PGRs and ECRs. Actively interacting with non-experts, such as school children, local communities, councils, charities, businesses or policy makers, who can ask the most innocent and awkward questions, can and does challenge your thinking and aids the research process. The benefits of engagement for the public, individual researchers and also for research are well known. For example, the number of research projects in which the public are involved, and not simply contributing to, online is phenomenal (from counting galaxies to the New Forest cicada).

There are numerous ways in which to engage with the public: giving a talk to a non-academic audience; helping with summer schools within your institution; engaging with the media; blogging/offering advice or support online, etc. The range of activity is as various as the researchers involved in it; the only limit is your imagination (and project management skills!). While all of this activity enhances your CV, it also enhances the reputation of your institution and is seen as good citizenship behaviour. Where this activity has an international dimension, even virtually from blogging, it will be seen as global citizenship. We would encourage every researcher to look at their research and what it can do in terms of the obvious outputs (a thesis, conference presentations, papers, grant applications and so on) and also explore their wider practitioner role. Can your research practice make a difference politically, culturally, socially and/or economically?

REFLECTION POINT

What new audience could you communicate your research to and inspire?

Enterprise and social enterprise

While the perception is that 'enterprise' is about turning research into business or money-making ventures, which may only have limited appeal, the idea of social enterprise should attract everyone because it is about making a difference in the world but in a slightly different way from public engagement above. The notion that enterprise is profit-driven is somewhat narrowly defined; our ideas should not only be published, but be implemented, preferably for the public (or global) good. Most universities have an enterprise or business unit or staff who will be able to advise you on collaborating with industry, creating spin-out companies, patents or setting up a business venture.

Social enterprise seeks to generate business but in a not-for-profit or ethical way. As the Social Enterprise UK says:

> Social enterprises are businesses that trade to tackle social problems, improve communities, people's life chances, or the environment. They make their money from selling goods and services in the open market, but they reinvest their profits back into the business or the local community. And so when they profit, society profits. (www.socialenterprise.org.uk/about (retrieved 14/4/2013))

REFLECTION POINT

How might your research benefit others? Could it create jobs, support the non-profit sector, make a financial contribution to the university? The challenge is to look at your research from a different perspective to see if you can find alternative applications.

Remember that in building your CV it is important to experiment, be adaptable and flexible: as Louis Pasteur said, '... chance ... favours the prepared mind'.

Continuous professional development (CPD)

By the end of any research project you will have acquired a considerable range of skills, but you will also need to have a heightened self-awareness (reflexivity) of what these skills are and at which standard you possess them, to be able to use them as the basis for your next career step. By taking advantage of the great opportunities universities offer, you will not only be adding to your CV and your repertoire of experience; you will also be growing and polishing the transferable skills you have acquired as a researcher. We believe this is critical because the PGR and ECR are in transitioning roles. You are at the beginning of a career path but may not have secured it or even firmly decided on its direction. Therefore, it is important to experiment in a safe and supportive environment and stretch yourself, testing out your skills with public engagement activities, enterprise, placements and secondments if possible. Consider what we say in Activity 11.2.

ACTIVITY 11.2   TEST YOURSELF

How will you know if you are a good leader unless you test your leadership skills? How will you know what your people management skills and style are unless you try them out? Universities are fantastic environments for 'experimenting with possible selves', as described by Herminia Ibarra (2003). What possible self would you like to try out this year?

We have suggested during the course of this book that, as a consequence of research work, you should have acquired a range of intellectual and information (detailed in Chapters 4 and 5) and practical project skills (detailed in Chapter 6), and, in addition, developed your interpersonal skills and personal effectiveness (detailed in Chapter 7). Although researchers find themselves in a very rich developmental environment, we suggest that engaging in research merely affords an individual an encounter with the skills we discussed. What brings these skills to life and into individual consciousness/self-awareness and, therefore, makes them transferable, is having the opportunity to explore and reflect on these skills, preferably guided by an expert. We discussed a range of methods for acquiring transferable skills in Chapter 3 whereas we set the context for the need for skills development in Chapter 1 and advised on how to identify your development needs in Chapter 2. We placed the researcher development agenda into context to indicate why people like us are passionate about your early career development.

Once acquired, however, your transferable skill set will undoubtedly require further work and refinement to improve it and ensure it continues to grow. You will need to push yourself round Kolb's learning cycle (Chapter 3) many times, reflecting on how well you are progressing and developing in relation to comparisons of your TNA/DNA/LNA results and your professional (long- or short-term) aspirations. The transferable skills you glean from your current research are only the beginning of an exciting journey. By definition, being a professional means continually reviewing and revising your skill set to ensure it is up to date and you are the best researcher/academic/manager, etc. you can be. Self-awareness, then, is a critical element of your *continuous (or continual) professional development* or CPD. Your learning will be driven by your professional needs and career ambitions; even if you do not seek promotion, you would still need CPD to remain current in the workplace.

We would count CPD as the final transferable skill researchers should have acquired as part of their development throughout their research projects. Establishing or carving out 'development time' is vital to your career progress. We hope this book has encouraged you to make the most of opportunities available now and in the future so that the habit of acquiring transferable skills as a researcher becomes an integral part of professional life. Some of you are already well underway: below we conclude with a quotation from a master's student responding to a question in a national committee about why anyone would want to study for a doctorate:

In October 2013 I will begin a PhD in Philosophy at the University of Glasgow. I have decided to embark on doctoral research for two reasons. Firstly, I enjoy reading and writing about philosophy, and feel passionately about the research topic I have proposed. Secondly, I am confident that the doctoral qualification will enhance my employability, and not only within academia. At the foundation of PhD research are core transferable intellectual skills: critical thinking, problem-solving and working effectively under pressurised time-constraints. These are vital skills for almost all working environments. Completing postgraduate research requires a strong work-ethic, determination and persistence, with long hours of independent study and unfaltering personal responsibility for one's own work. At the same time, doctoral students often tutor or lecture undergraduates, developing leadership and teaching skills, and will participate in numerous organising committees, honing team-work and networking abilities. The 'Graduate Conference' organising committee is a good example of academic skills transferred to a 'business' environment: event management, financial budgets, fundraising, advertising, hospitality and email management. Not only does PhD study allow for original academic research, but it provides a platform to develop and hone the transferable skills needed to succeed in almost any working environment, creating a well-rounded and highly employable individual. This is why I consider my PhD study not as a niche specialisation, but as an opportunity to widen my skill set in preparation for my future career.

Catherine Robb, HEA Student Advisor

Ideas for further reading

Becker, L. and Denicolo, P. (2013) *Success in Research: Teaching in Higher Education*. London: Sage.

Bolles, R.N. (2013) *What Color is Your Parachute? A Practical Manual for Job-Hunters and Career-Changers* (revised and updated annually). New York: Ten Speed Press.

Denicolo, P. (ed.) (2013) *Success in Research: Achieving Impact in Research*. London: Sage.

Denicolo, P. and Becker, L. (2012) *Success in Research: Developing Research Proposals*. London: Sage.

Doyle-Morris S. (2009) *Beyond the Boys' Club: Strategies for Achieving Career Success as a Woman Working in a Male Dominated Field*. Milton Keynes: Wit and Wisdom Press. See also S. Doyle-Morris blog: Femalebreadwinners.com.

Ibarra, I. (2003) *Working Identity: Unconventional Strategies for Reinventing Your Career*. Boston, MA: Harvard Business School Publishing.

Leyser, O. (2011) *Mothers in Science: 64 Ways to Have it All*. London: The Royal Society. Available online at: http://royalsociety.org/uploadedFiles/Royal_Society_Content/about-us/equality/2011-06-15-Mothers-in-Science.pdf (retrieved 14/4/2013).

Shein, E.H. (2006) *Career Anchors: Self Assessment* (3rd edition). San Francisco, CA: John Wiley & Sons.

The Royal Society (2010) *The Scientific Century: Securing Our Future Prosperity* (policy document). London: The Royal Society.

The National Coordinating Centre for Public Engagement website contains lots of useful information, ideas and advice at: www.publicengagement.ac.uk/ (retrieved 14/4/2013).

The Social Enterprise UK website contains useful information, ideas and advice at: www.socialenterprise.org.uk/ (retrieved 14/4/2013).

APPENDIX 1

JOINT STATEMENT SKILLS (JSS)

Skills training requirements for research students: joint statement by the research councils/Arts and Humanities Research Board – 2001 (JSS)

Introduction

The research councils and the Arts and Humanities Research Board (AHRB) play an important role in setting standards and identifying best practice in research training. This document sets out a joint statement of the skills that doctoral research students funded by the research councils/ AHRB would be expected to develop during their research training.

These skills may be present on commencement, explicitly taught, or developed during the course of the research. It is expected that different mechanisms will be used to support learning as appropriate, including self-direction, supervisor support and mentoring, departmental support, workshops, conferences, elective training courses, formally assessed courses and informal opportunities.

The research councils and the AHRB would also want to re-emphasise their belief that training in research skills and techniques is the key element in the development of a research student, and that PhD students are expected to make a substantial, original contribution to knowledge in their area, normally leading to published work. The development of wider employment-related skills should not detract from that core objective.

The purpose of this statement is to give a common view of the skills and experience of a typical research student, thereby providing universities with a clear and consistent message aimed at helping them to ensure that all research training is of the highest standard, across all disciplines. It is not the intention of this document to provide assessment criteria for research training.

It is expected that each council/board will have additional requirements specific to their field of interest and will continue to have their own measures for the evaluation of research training within institutions.

(A) Research skills and techniques – to be able to demonstrate:

1. The ability to recognise and validate problems and to formulate and test hypotheses.
2. Original, independent and critical thinking, and the ability to develop theoretical concepts.
3. A knowledge of recent advances within one's field and in related areas.
4. An understanding of relevant research methodologies and techniques and their appropriate application within one's research field.
5. The ability to analyse critically and evaluate one's findings and those of others.
6. An ability to summarise, document, report and reflect on progress.

(B) Research environment – to be able to:

1. Show a broad understanding of the context, at the national and international level, in which research takes place.
2. Demonstrate awareness of issues relating to the rights of other researchers, of research subjects, and of others who may be affected by the research, e.g. confidentiality, ethical issues, attribution, copyright, malpractice, ownership of data and the requirements of the Data Protection Act.
3. Demonstrate appreciation of standards of good research practice in their institution and/or discipline.
4. Understand relevant health and safety issues and demonstrate responsible working practices.
5. Understand the processes for funding and evaluation of research.
6. Justify the principles and experimental techniques used in one's own research.
7. Understand the process of academic or commercial exploitation of research results.

(C) Research management – to be able to:

1. Apply effective project management through the setting of research goals, intermediate milestones and prioritisation of activities.
2. Design and execute systems for the acquisition and collation of information through the effective use of appropriate resources and equipment.
3. Identify and access appropriate bibliographical resources, archives, and other sources of relevant information. Use information technology appropriately for database management, recording and presenting information.

(D) Personal effectiveness – to be able to:

1. Demonstrate a willingness and ability to learn and acquire knowledge.
2. Be creative, innovative and original in one's approach to research.
3. Demonstrate flexibility and open-mindedness.
4. Demonstrate self-awareness and the ability to identify own training needs.
5. Demonstrate self-discipline, motivation, and thoroughness.
6. Recognise boundaries and draw upon/use sources of support as appropriate.
7. Show initiative, work independently and be self-reliant.

(E) Communication skills – to be able to:

1. Write clearly and in a style appropriate to purpose, e.g. progress reports, published documents, thesis.
2. Construct coherent arguments and articulate ideas clearly to a range of audiences, formally and informally through a variety of techniques.
3. Constructively defend research outcomes at seminars and viva examination.
4. Contribute to promoting the public understanding of one's research field.
5. Effectively support the learning of others when involved in teaching, mentoring or demonstrating activities.

(F) Networking and team working – to be able to:

1. Develop and maintain co-operative networks and working relationships with supervisors, colleagues and peers, within the institution and the wider research community.
2. Understand one's behaviours and impact on others when working in and contributing to the success of formal and informal teams.
3. Listen, give and receive feedback and respond perceptively to others.

(G) Career management – to be able to:

1. Appreciate the need for and show commitment to continued professional development.
2. Take ownership for and manage one's career progression, set realistic and achievable career goals, and identify and develop ways to improve employability.
3. Demonstrate an insight into the transferable nature of research skills to other work environments and the range of career opportunities within and outside academia.
4. Present one's skills, personal attributes and experiences through effective CVs, applications and interviews.

APPENDIX 2
DEVELOPMENT CYCLE DIAGRAM

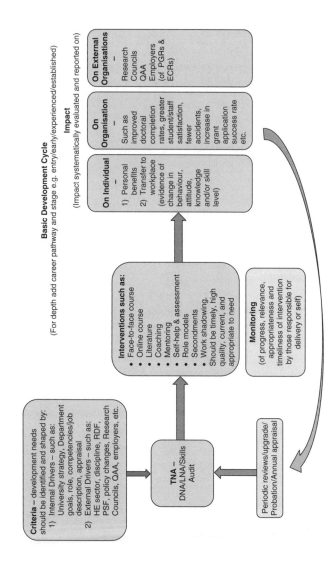

FIGURE A.2

APPENDIX 3

SUMMARY DIAGRAM OF THE RESEARCHER DEVELOPMENT FRAMEWORK

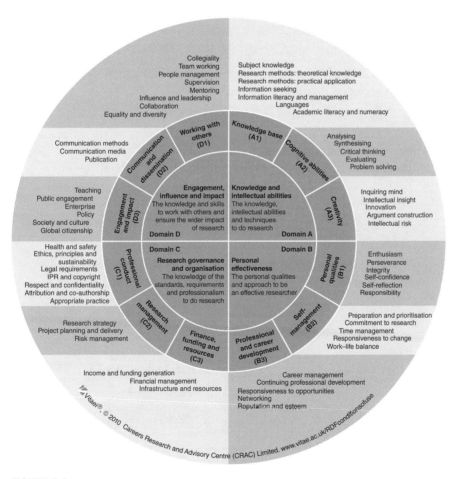

FIGURE A.3

Reprinted with the kind permission of Vitae

APPENDIX 4

EMPLOYABILITY SKILLS QUESTIONNAIRE

Reprinted with the kind permission of Janet Pink, Janet Pink Training Coaching & Consultancy, and adapted from *Employability Skills 2000+* by The Conference Board of Canada.

Listed below are the fundamental skills that employers say are needed to enter, remain, and progress in today's workplace.

Rate yourself against each employability skill as follows:

1. I'm not as skilled as I'd like
2. I'm skilled
3. I'm very skilled

Communicating   1   2   3

I read and understand information presented in a variety of forms (e.g., words, graphs, charts, diagrams)

I write and speak so others pay attention and understand

I listen and ask questions to understand and appreciate the points of view of others

I share information using a range of information and communications technologies (e.g., voice, email, computers)

I use relevant scientific, technological and mathematical knowledge and skills to explain or clarify ideas

Managing Information   1   2   3

I locate, gather and organise information using appropriate technology and information systems

I access, analyse and apply knowledge and explain or clarify ideal skills from various disciplines (e.g., the arts, languages, science, technology, mathematics, social sciences, and the humanities)

Using Numbers   1   2   3

I decide what needs to be measured or calculated

I observe and record data using appropriate methods, tools and technology

Thinking & Problem Solving   1   2   3

I assess situations and identify problems

I seek different points of view and evaluate them based on facts

I recognise the human, interpersonal, technical, scientific and mathematical dimensions of a problem

I identify the root cause of a problem

I am creative and innovative in exploring possible solutions

I readily use science, technology and mathematics as ways to think, gain and share knowledge, solve problems and make decisions.

I evaluate solutions to make recommendations or decisions

I implement solutions

I check to see if a solution works, and act on opportunities for improvement

Working with Others   1   2   3

I understand and work within the dynamics of a group

I ensure that a team's purpose and objectives are clear

I recognise and respect people's diversity, individual differences and perspectives, and am open to and supportive of the thoughts, opinions and contributions of others in a group.

I accept and provide feedback in a constructive and considerate manner

I contribute to a team by sharing information and expertise

I lead or support when appropriate, motivating a group for high performance

I understand the role of conflict in a group to reach solutions

I manage and resolve conflict when appropriate

Participate in Projects & Tasks   1   2   3

I plan, design or carry out a project or task from start to finish with well-defined objectives and outcomes

I develop a plan, seek feedback, test, revise and implement

I work to agreed quality standards and specifications

I select and use appropriate tools and technology for a task or project

I adapt to changing requirements and information

I continuously monitor the success of a project or task and identify ways to improve

Demonstrate Positive Attitudes & Behaviours   1   2   3

Feel good about yourself and be confident

I deal with people, problems and situations with honesty, integrity and personal ethics

I recognise my own and other people's positive efforts

I take care of my personal health and well-being

I show interest, initiative and demonstrate effort

Be Adaptable   1   2   3

I work independently or as a part of a team

I carry out multiple tasks or projects

I am innovative and resourceful: identify and suggest alternative ways to achieve goals and get the job done

I am open and embrace change

I learn from my mistakes, and accept and act on feedback

I demonstrate resilience and cope with uncertainty

Continuously Learn & Develop   1   2   3

I am willing to continuously learn and grow

I assess personal strengths and areas for development

I set my own learning goals

I identify and access learning sources and opportunities

I plan for and achieve learning goals

Work Safely   1   2   3

I am aware of personal and group health and safety practices and procedures, and act in accordance with these

GLOSSARY OF TERMS

How they are used in this book.

Action learning set – a small informal group of people who discuss real problems or a group member's work-related issues without being judgemental. Some groups have a facilitator and some are self-facilitating.

Appraisal – a formal review of an individual's performance at work, usually held on annual basis; used to monitor progress, assesses previous activity and contributions, agree future activity/objectives, and identify any training required to fulfil the objectives.

360 degree appraisal – gathers feedback from a professional's senior managers, peers and subordinates, and clients if appropriate.

Attribute(s) – quality, ability, skill, ascribed to an individual.

Competence(s) – an individual's ability to do something usually associated with an expected standard or level of performance or behaviour.

Development – gradual unfolding or progress of an individual or specific attribute.

Employability – a person's level of capabilities that will make them attractive to prospective employers; the skill set and attributes that enhance a person's prospects of gaining employment.

Field – term for specialist research sphere and/or subject area.

Huddles – people gather round (huddle) in a close circle for a short and brief meeting (10–15 minutes), usually held standing up to focus attention.

Impact and Evaluation Group – an advisory group to the HE sector on how to measure the effectiveness of training and development.

Learning outcome – the aim or purpose of a course or programme; what participants can expect to gain from participating in a course or programme.

Learning styles – preferences or approach to learning.

Logs – records kept in a book or list-form common in STEMM areas; an old and well-known format is a ship's log book that provides a record of voyages.

Metadata – data about data.

Professional profile – a personal description of attributes which make one suitable for employment, including knowledge, qualifications, skills and personal qualities.

Public engagement – activity that involves 'the public' in research and/or shares research with non-academic people and organisations, such as schools, business, charities, government bodies, and so on.

Research Excellence Framework (REF) – a process of expert review for assessing the quality of research in UK Higher Education institutions.

Skill – a practised ability or specific expertise.

Transfer – the formal registration process by which a researcher moves into the role of doctoral researcher, perhaps from an MPhil degree; can also be known as the upgrade process and is equivalent to a confirmation of study at that level.

Unique Selling Point (USP) – derived from marketing, a special quality or characteristic that differentiates an individual and can be used to illustrate and promote their distinctive characteristics or skill set (especially to a prospective employer).

Upgrade – see *Transfer*

INDEX